The Salem Witch Trials

Other books in the At Issue in History series:

The Salem Witch Trials

Laura Marvel, *Book Editor*

Daniel Leone, *President*
Bonnie Szumski, *Publisher*
Scott Barbour, *Managing Editor*
James D. Torr, *Series Editor*

OPPOSING VIEWPOINTS® SERIES **AT ISSUE IN HISTORY**

GREENHAVEN
PRESS®

THOMSON
—★—™
GALE

San Diego • Detroit • New York • San Francisco • Cleveland
New Haven, Conn. • Waterville, Maine • London • Munich

THOMSON
—————*————— ™
GALE

Cover credit: © Bettmann/CORBIS
Library of Congress, 97
North Wind Picture Archives, 59, 121

LIBRARY OF CONGRESS CATALOGING-IN-PUBLICATION DATA
Salem witch trials / Laura Marvel, book editor.
p. cm. — (At issue in history)
Includes bibliographical references and index.
ISBN 0-7377-0822-0 (pbk. : alk. paper) — ISBN 0-7377-0823-9 (alk. paper)
1. Witchcraft—Massachusetts—Salem—History—17th century—Juvenile litera-
ture. [1. Witchcraft—Massachusetts—Salem. 2. Salem (Mass.)—History—Colonial
period, ca. 1600–1775.] I. Marvel, Laura. II. Series.
BF1576 .S24 2003
133.4'3'097445—dc21   2001008518

Printed in the United States of America

Contents

the betrayer of Christ, thus fueling suspicion in
the community.

Chapter 2: What Motivated the "Afflicted" Girls?

Chapter 3: Why Would the Innocent Confess?

Foreword

Historian Robert Weiss defines history simply as "a record and interpretation of past events." Both elements—record and interpretation—are necessary, Weiss argues.

> Names, dates, places, and events are the essence of history. But historical writing is not a compendium of facts. It consists of facts placed in a sequence to tell a connected story. A work of history is not merely a story, however. It also must analyze what happened and *why*—that is, it must interpret the past for the reader.

For example, the events of December 7, 1941, that led President Franklin D. Roosevelt to call it "a date which will live in infamy" are fairly well known and straightforward. A force of Japanese planes and submarines launched a torpedo and bombing attack on American military targets in Pearl Harbor, Hawaii. The surprise assault sank five battleships, disabled or sank fourteen additional ships, and left almost twenty-four hundred American soldiers and sailors dead. On the following day, the United States formally entered World War II when Congress declared war on Japan.

These facts and consequences were almost immediately communicated to the American people who heard reports about Pearl Harbor and President Roosevelt's response on the radio. All realized that this was an important and pivotal event in American and world history. Yet the news from Pearl Harbor raised many unanswered questions. Why did Japan decide to launch such an offensive? Why were the attackers so successful in catching America by surprise? What did the attack reveal about the two nations, their people, and their leadership? What were its causes, and what were its effects? Political leaders, academic historians, and students look to learn the basic facts of historical events and to read the intepretations of these events by many different sources, both primary and secondary, in order to develop a more complete picture of the event in a historical context.

In the case of Pearl Harbor, several important questions surrounding the event remain in dispute, most notably the role of President Roosevelt. Some historians have blamed his policies for deliberately provoking Japan to attack in order to propel America into World War II; a few have gone so far as to accuse him of knowing of the impending attack but not informing others. Other historians, examining the same event, have exonerated the president of such charges, arguing that the historical evidence does not support such a theory.

The Greenhaven At Issue in History series recognizes that many important historical events have been interpreted differently and in some cases remain shrouded in controversy. Each volume features a collection of articles that focus on a topic that has sparked controversy among eyewitnesses, contemporary observers, and historians. An introductory essay sets the stage for each topic by presenting background and context. Several chapters then examine different facets of the subject at hand with readings chosen for their diversity of opinion. Each selection is preceded by a summary of the author's main points and conclusions. A bibliography is included for those students interested in pursuing further research. An annotated table of contents and thorough index help readers to quickly locate material of interest. Taken together, the contents of each of the volumes in the Greenhaven At Issue in History series will help students become more discriminating and thoughtful readers of history.

Introduction

The word "Salem," an ancient form of Jerusalem, means peace, but for most Americans today the name Salem evokes the site of the infamous witch trials. No witches were dramatically burned at the stake in America (as condemned witches had been in Europe), but the events in 1692 in Salem, Massachusetts, continue to haunt Americans with images of hysterical accusations, fear, and panic. The actual number of executions in Salem was small compared to the casualties of some European witch-hunts, but the proceedings of the courts that condemned twenty women and men to death continue to trouble Americans who value a system of justice which presumes innocence until guilt is proven. Why was there a witch-hunt in 1692 in a village whose name means peace? What motivated the "afflicted" girls who were the chief accusers of witches? How did the court system err so miserably? Historians, sociologists, psychologists, and writers have offered various interpretations of these critical issues, and scholars continue to unearth details and formulate theories that may shed new light on the crisis.

Witch-Hunts in Europe

In many ways the story of the Salem witch-hunt begins in Europe. Historian Brian P. Levack explains that the great European witch-hunts stretched from 1450 to 1750, involved thousands of victims, and were a result of "new ideas about witches and a series of fundamental changes in the criminal law" as well as "both religious change and social tension."[1] What made possible full-scale witch-hunts was not just belief in witches who practiced black magic to work harm on others, but the connection made by the educated Christian elite linking magic to devil worship. According to Levack, "The emergence of the belief that witches were not merely magicians but Devil-worshippers changed the nature of the crime of witchcraft. It made witches not simply felons, similar to murderers and thieves, but heretics and apostates, intrinsically evil individuals who had rejected

11

their Christian faith and had decided instead to serve God's enemy, the Devil." The critical changes in criminal procedure at the time involved a movement to the inquisitorial system, where judges initiated proceedings, and the new ability of the court to order torture to gain both confessions and the names of other witches.

Religious and social changes during the early sixteenth century intensified witch-hunts. Reformers such as Martin Luther and John Calvin emphasized the presence of the devil in the world and encouraged a declaration of war against him. These reformers also instituted a new focus on intense personal scrutiny to discover the true state of one's soul. At times such scrutiny led to a sense of personal guilt which could be relieved only by projecting the guilt onto others, ideally a witch.

Women's position within society made them particularly vulnerable to accusations of witchcraft. Considered intellectually inferior and sexually insatiable, women's roles as cooks, healers, and midwives made them particularly suspect. Cooks had the opportunity to gather herbs and the skill to turn them into potions. Herbs were also central to folk remedies for healing, and belief in these folk remedies was tied up with other superstitions about magic. Midwives, who made use of unguents and lotions, were vulnerable to accusations of intentional infanticide. In addition, sexually experienced women were a special threat to men's sense of superiority when it became widely recognized that women were more ardent and sexually capable than men as both reach old age. Levack explains that objects of "male sexual fear" became objects of "male accusations of witchcraft."[3] The poor, old, and powerless members of society were also easy scapegoats, especially if they were also grouchy and bitter.

Levack notes that there was a general sense of anxiety about inflation, famine and plague, religious dissent, popular rebellions, the spread of poverty, and even the emergence of capitalism. This anxiety led to fear among both laborers and the learned and ruling classes that society was disintegrating because of Satan's presence. Witch-hunting was a way to release this anxiety. A witch-hunt was usually triggered by a personal misfortune or a community disaster. Large-scale witch-hunts (involving ten to three hundred victims) often ended when the wealthy and powerful began to be accused.

According to Creighton University professor Bryan F. LeBeau, "England had lower rates of prosecution and execution of witches than did most other countries in Europe" because "judges did not initiate cases, neighbors did,"[4] and because the courts were not allowed to use torture to secure confessions. LeBeau notes that witch trials in England "were often an outgrowth of community conflict. They arose out of quarreling between neighbors, often over loans and gifts, followed by oral outbursts and subsequent unexpected misfortune suffered by one of the parties."[5] The one full-scale witch-hunt in England occurred during the English civil war, as Royalists and Puritans vied for control of Parliament. Matthew Hopkins, a lawyer operating through a "special commission of Oyer and Terminer," led in the prosecution of fifty witches in Essex County, England, between 1645 and 1646.

The Massachusetts Bay Colony

Nearly fifty years after the witch-hunt in Essex County, England, Essex County, Massachusetts, became the site of America's most notorious witch-hunt. The original Massachusetts Bay Colony settlers arrived in the 1630s. They were English Puritans determined to create what their first governor, John Winthrop, called "A City on a Hill"[6]: a utopian theocracy dedicated to God and determined to be a model of pure Christian piety. There was no separation between church and state in the colony, and it was accepted that hierarchical order was God's intention. Some would be high, some low, some rich, some poor. It was equally accepted that women were subordinate to men. Willing acceptance of one's place in the hierarchy was an act of love which strengthened the ligaments necessary to make the body of the community perfect, according to Winthrop.

The Puritans brought with them to the New World a clear sense of the power of the great enemy, the Devil, who was likely to tempt and test God's new chosen people more rigorously than ordinary Christians. They also brought a strongly Calvinist theology which encouraged intense scrutiny of one's own life, thoughts, and impulses to determine whether one was a member of the elect or incurably reprobate. The original settlers also carried with them from England a belief in witches as practitioners of black magic and as servants of the devil. Governor Winthrop records in his journal his suspicion in 1637 that Jane Hawkins, an out-spoken woman who tested his authority, was a witch. He also comments briefly on Alice Young, the first person exe-cuted as a witch in New England (in 1647), and he com-ments extensively on Margaret Jones, who was executed in 1648 as a witch.

As the colony grew and expanded it began to experience the kinds of political, social, and religious disruptions which had provided fertile soil for witch-hunts in Europe. Epi-demics of diseases such as smallpox, measles, and influenza, devastating hurricanes and fires, intensified hostilities with the Indians, the revocation of the colony charter, and the economic change from an agricultural colony to a commer-cial society created high levels of anxiety and frustration in the colony. Ministers began to warn parishioners that God was punishing the people for slackening their religious commitment, and many attributed their sense of dislocation to the active presence of the devil in New England.

Why a Witch-Hunt in Salem?

Within this general context of change and anxiety, Salem Vil-lage was experiencing specific difficulties. In spite of its name, it was hardly a haven of tranquillity. Amherst professors Paul Boyer and Stephen Nissenbaum note that "for years its 600-odd residents had been divided into two bitterly antagonistic

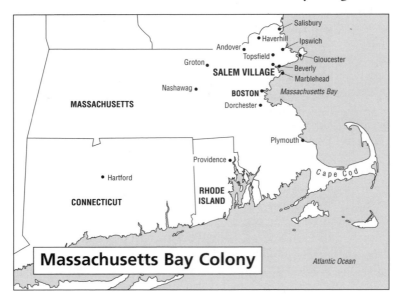

factions."[7] One, led by the Putnam family, wanted Salem Village to separate from nearby Salem Town; the other, with strong commercial ties to Salem Town, was unwilling to support a separate Salem Village community. These factions had not been reconciled by the first three ministers called to the village, and the fourth, Reverend Samuel Parris, a thirty-six-year-old merchant turned minister, sided with the Putnams and escalated the conflict. In October of 1691, the anti-Parris contingent gained control of the Village Committee. Reverend Parris claimed he felt the presence of the devil threatening the peace of the village.

That winter, several neighborhood girls between the ages of nine and twenty began gathering and apparently experimenting with charms and fortune-telling. Perhaps the children in the Parris and Putnam households were directed in their experiments by Reverend Parris's West Indian servant, Tituba. Perhaps they simply became frightened and upset by their fortunes. At any rate, four girls (Elizabeth Parris, Abigail Williams, Elizabeth Hubbard, and Ann Putnam) began exhibiting alarming physical symptoms, and soon several other girls were also afflicted. The neighborhood physician, Dr. William Griggs, is normally credited with diagnosing the afflicted girls as being "under the Evil Hand," or bewitched. Shortly after this diagnosis, the girls identified their afflicters, and three women were arrested as witches: Sarah Good, Sarah Osborne, and Tituba. By the end of the summer at least 160 people had been arrested and jailed for witchcraft.

Perhaps the accusations were motivated by factional politics rather than mass hysteria, as historian Enders A. Robinson argues. Perhaps Reverend Parris's response to the girls' behavior (public fasts and prayers) as well as his sermon in March suggesting that church members as well as derelicts could be witches, moved the crisis from a small incident to a major witch-hunt, as historian Larry Gragg suggests. No doubt a complex combination of general anxiety, specific village problems, unnatural behavior on the part of the girls, and the responses of the adults in the community all contributed to the crisis.

The Accusers and the Accused

The nature of the girls' afflictions had received considerable attention. Reverend John Hale, from nearby Beverly, described their affliction as follows: "These Children were bitten and pinched by invisible agents; their arms, necks, and backs turned this way and that way, and returned back again, so as it was impossible for them to do of themselves, and beyond the power of any Epileptick Fits, or natural Disease to effect."[8] These convulsions, the sensations of being pricked and bitten, their screeching and screaming in the courtroom, their vocal disruption of normal church services, and their ability to see disembodied specters, have led eyewitnesses and later scholars to a variety of interpretations. In 1692, according to historian David Harley, the ministers were divided between believing the girls bewitched, in which case they were relatively innocent victims of witches, and believing them possessed by the Devil, in which case the girls' guilty souls were in jeopardy, and their testimony could be seen as malevolently guided by the Devil.

Until well into the twentieth century, the girls were considered actresses: Charles W. Upham suggests that they pretended their afflictions in order to gain attention. When the situation got out of hand, they continued to pretend in order to avoid being accused of making false accusations. More recently the girls' behavior has been attributed to hysteria, intergenerational conflict and displaced aggression, psychological projection of anger and frustration, and social discontent. A PBS special, *Secrets of the Dead: The Witches' Curse*, traces the theory first proposed by behavioral psychologist Linnda R. Caporael in 1976 that the girls' convulsions and hallucinations may have resulted from ergot poisoning. Ergot is a fungus which grows on grains, including rye, and could thus infect rye bread. Although this theory has been disputed by Carleton psychologists Nicholas P. Spanos and Jack Gottlieb, the possibility that some form of poisoning caused the girls' initial physical symptoms, if not their subsequent behavior in court, remains intriguing.

Those women initially accused of witchcraft fit, to some degree, a general profile: They were powerless women with suspect pasts. Tituba, with her West Indian heritage and her position as a servant, was an easy target. Sarah Good, a member of the landless poor as a result of the debt accrued by her husbands, seemed to grumble when denied charity and looked like the eccentric, outspoken, melancholic woman the girls might expect to be a witch. Sarah Osborne, who had married her Irish indentured servant after the death of her first husband, was involved in a lawsuit with the sons of her first marriage over the property left by her first husband. Martha Corey, though a respectable member of the church, had given birth to an illegitimate mulatto child who still lived with her and her current husband, Giles Corey.

Soon the accusations broadened to include respectable women like Rebecca Nurse (the seventy-one-year-old matriarch whose rising prosperity may have annoyed some village members), Nurse's sisters, Mary Easty and Sarah Cloyce, and other respectable men and women like John and Elizabeth Proctor, the wealthy merchant Philip English, and a former minister of the Salem Village church, Reverend George Burroughs. Respectable women and men, children and clergy, the wealthy and the witless were quickly added to the growing lists of the accused. The witch-hunt also broadened geographically, extending to the neighboring towns of Andover, Beverly, Topsfield, and Reading.

Trials and Executions

Paul Boyer and Stephen Nissenbaum have gathered in three volumes a significant body of documents relating to the witch trials, including depositions, petitions, and reports of the initial hearings presided over by Judges Hathorne and Corwin. The actual records of the trials held before the Court of Oyer and Terminer have vanished, however. Governor Phips had established the court on May 27, 1962, specifically to hear the witchcraft cases, but scholars must piece together the proceedings based on the accounts of the initial hearings, narratives of eyewitnesses, and notes of the court clerks. Specifically at issue is the nature of the evidence accepted by the court which led to the convictions. As Boyer and Nissenbaum explain, the chief problem was that "the evil deeds on which the indictments rested were not perpetrated by the witches at all, but by intangible spirits who could at times assume their shape."[9] In other words, the evil deeds were perpetrated by specters. Since the specters were only visible to those making the accusations, spectral evidence was exceptionally difficult to either verify or disprove. As a result, the magistrates resorted to all manner of corroborating empirical evidence to support the spectral evidence.

Such empirical evidence consisted of proof of the accused person's supernatural attributes (for example, feats of strength or mindreading), evidence of a witch's tit (described by Boyer and Nissenbaum as "an abnormal physical ap-

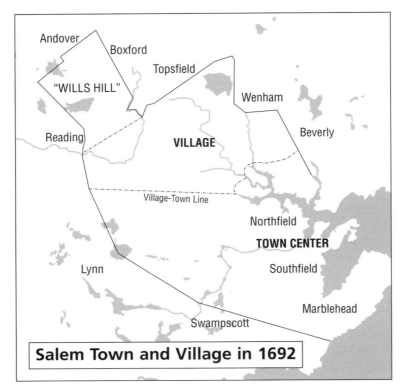

Salem Town and Village in 1692

pendage, ordinarily quite small, through which a witch or wizard was thought to give suck to the devil in the form of a bird, a turtle, or some other small creature"[10]), and such tests as recitation of the Lord's Prayer (witches supposedly would recite the prayer inaccurately) and the sight and touch test (to determine whether the gaze of the accused witch would send the afflicted girls into fits and whether the touch of the accused witch would stop the fit). Evidence of demonic mischief (a curse or an evil gaze which caused misfortune for the accuser) was also used to corroborate a charge of witchcraft, but the cause-and-effect relationship was often difficult to prove beyond doubt. As a result, confession became the strongest and most acceptable form of evidence.

The pressure exerted by the court and community for confessions was difficult to withstand and many succumbed to the pressure who later recanted their confessions. Ironically, confession, which should have led immediately to conviction, in fact led to a reprieve, perhaps because confessing witches were held to testify against others, or perhaps because the judges believed confession to be the first step toward reformation and reconciliation with God. Those who adamantly insisted on their innocence—and who questioned the girls' veracity and the nature of the evidence accepted by the court—were the ones who were convicted and executed.

The Court of Oyer and Terminer convened five times, convicted twenty-seven women and men, and executed nineteen by hanging on four separate days: June 10, July 19, August 19, September 22. Giles Corey refused to stand trial and was pressed to death on September 19. Six women were reprieved for pregnancy or confession; one woman escaped before being executed. The court was dismissed by Governor Phips on October 29. According to historian Larry Gragg, spectral evidence and the sight and touch test were being scorned by knowledgeable authorities, and the validity of the testimony of both the afflicted girls and the confessing witches was being questioned by many. Other factors, such as Reverend Increase Mather's cautions about spectral evidence and the condition of the girls, may also have influenced Phips to dismiss the court. The Superior Court of Judicature was formed in December 1692 to hear the remaining cases. Four of the judges who had served the Court of Oyer and Terminer, including Samuel Sewall, were appointed to the Superior Court. The Superior Court heard fifty-two cases; it acquitted forty-nine of the defendants and convicted three, who were immediately pardoned by Governor Phips.

Governor Phips pardoned those accused who remained in jail in the early months of 1693; Reverend Parris, Judge Samuel Sewall, the twelve jurors who had served the Court of Oyer and Terminer, and Ann Putnam, one of the "afflicted" girls, all repented their actions in the years that followed the crisis. Some monetary restitution was made to the families of the victims in 1710, and the sentences of twenty-two of the convicted were reversed in 1711. Not until the mid–twentieth century, however, were the names of the remaining victims cleared by an act of the Massachusetts legislature. In 1992, on the three hundredth anniversary of the trials, a monument was erected in Salem to honor those who went to their deaths insisting their innocence.

The Salem witch crisis has captured the imaginations of countless students and scholars, and such notable writers as Nathaniel Hawthorne in the nineteenth century and Arthur Miller in the twentieth have wrestled with the incident in fiction and drama. Hawthorne, an ancestor of both Judge William Hathorne, who presided over the initial hearings, and Philip English, one of the accused, explored his own family history in relation to the historical events in *The House of the Seven Gables* (1851). Miller's play *The Crucible* (1953) offers a controversial vision of the characters and condemnations of John Proctor, George Jacobs, Giles and Martha Corey, and Rebecca Nurse. It also offers startling interpretations of the afflicted girls' motivations and the actions of the judges and ministers while suggesting parallels between the events of 1692 and the anti-Communist witch-hunt of the 1950s.

Although Salem Village was incorporated as the town of Danvers, Massachusetts, in 1757, the events that began there in the winter of 1692 are inextricably connected to the pre-1757 town, Salem Village. These events continue to haunt the imaginations and trouble the minds of Americans over three hundred years later. The selections in this anthology are intended to help readers reconstruct the significance and meaning of the Salem witch trials.

Notes

1. Brian P. Levack, *The Witch-Hunt in Early Modern Europe*. London: Longman, 1987, p. 3.
2. Levack, *The Witch-Hunt in Early Modern Europe*, p. 8.
3. Levack, *The Witch-Hunt in Early Modern Europe*, p. 130.
4. Bryan F. LeBeau, *The Story of the Salem Witch Trials*. Upper Saddle River, NJ: Prentice-Hall, 1998, p. 18.
5. LeBeau, *The Story of the Salem Witch Trials*, p. 19.
6. John Winthrop, "A Model of Christian Charity" in *The Norton Anthology of American Literature*, 3rd. ed., ed. Nina Baym. New York: W.W. Norton, 1999, p. 118.
7. Paul Boyer and Stephen Nissenbaum, Introduction to *The Salem Witchcraft Papers*. New York: Da Capo Press, 1977, p. 5.
8. John Hale, "A Modest Inquiry into the Nature of Witchcraft," in *Narratives of the Witchcraft Cases, 1648–1706*, ed. George Lincoln Burr. Reprint. New York: Barnes & Noble, 1975, p. 413.
9. Paul Boyer and Stephen Nissenbaum, *Salem Possessed: The Social Origins of Witchcraft*. Cambridge, MA: Harvard University Press, 1974, p. 11.
10. Boyer and Nissenbaum, *Salem Possessed*, p. 13.

Chapter 1

Why a Witch-Hunt in Salem in 1692?

1

Theological and Political Conditions Made Salem Vulnerable

Richard Weisman

In this excerpt from his book, *Witchcraft, Magic, and Religion in 17th-Century Massachusetts*, political historian Richard Weisman outlines the events that occurred in Salem in 1692–1693; he then explains the theological and political conditions which made Salem vulnerable to this witchcraft crisis.

Established by royal charter in 1629 as a self-governing English colony, the Massachusetts Bay Colony considered itself a community of chosen people bound to God by a special covenant relationship. By 1690, however, many Puritan ministers in the colony were warning their congregations of the impending doom which their moral failings would provoke God to exact. In addition to this sense of failure as a community of saints, the colony was experiencing political anxiety over revocation of their royal charter in 1684, followed by a period of English rule by royally appointed "presidents," then negotiations over a new charter which undermined the Puritan sect's power. The intensified threat of Indian attack also contributed to a general fear that the colony would collapse. According to Weisman, the discovery of witchcraft in Salem at this time of social upheaval offered an explanation for the failings of the colony.

In early February 1692, several members and friends of the household of Samuel Parris, minister for Salem Village since 1689, were taken with strange fits. A local physi-

Excerpted from *Witchcraft, Magic, and Religion in 17th-Century Massachusetts*, by Richard Weisman (Amherst: The University of Massachusetts Press, 1984).

cian was summoned to examine Elizabeth, Parris's nine-year-old daughter; Abigail Williams, his eleven-year-old niece; and a few other girls and young women, all of whom complained of similar physical torments. Not unexpectedly, Dr. Griggs confirmed Parris's worst suspicions. The girls were victims of bewitchment.

Shortly thereafter, the youthful victims—or the afflicted, as they came to be designated by contemporaries—began to cry out the names of their tormentors. The first suspects were brought before local magistrates in Salem on February 29. Concurrent with these preliminary examinations, alternative nonlegal remedies were applied to the sufferings of the afflicted. A group of ministers congregated at Parris's residence for a solemn day of prayer on March 11. Also, one of the former ministers of Salem Village, Deodat Lawson, visited Parris a week later to offer his assistance. Neither of these attempts at intercession proved effective. The condition of the young women steadily deteriorated.

Eventually, a special court, the Court of Oyer and Terminer, was convened by the governor to sit in judgment over the alarming number of suspects now detained by the Salem magistrates. The Court of Oyer and Terminer was composed exclusively of prominent magistrates. When this body met for the first time on June 2, the ranks of the accused had swelled to over seventy men and women. The decision of the magistrates at their first formal session on June 10 defined the orientation of the court for the remainder of its existence. A verdict of guilty was turned in for the one suspect who was tried. In the next four meetings of the court, on June 30, August 5, September 9, and September 17, guilty verdicts were returned for all cases. By early October, fifty of the accused had confessed to the crime of witchcraft, another twenty-six had been convicted by the court, and, of these twenty-six condemned witches, nineteen had been executed. Moreover, there was reason to believe that the work of the Court of Oyer and Terminer had only just begun. The prisons of Boston, Salem, and Ipswich were filled to capacity with untried suspects. In addition, new allegations were filtering into the court each day.

Then, on October 12, in the midst of this apparently growing epidemic, Gov. William Phips, only recently appointed to his post, ordered a halt to the prosecutions. A new court was constituted on November 25 to replace the

General Court—formerly the highest court in the colony—and to preside over the remaining witchcraft cases. In four sessions held on January 2, January 31, April 25, and May of 1693, this court—The Superior Court of Judicature—reversed the policy of its predecessor. In the first session, held at Salem, the grand jury accepted indictments for only twenty-one of more than fifty persons awaiting trial. The magistrates returned verdicts of guilty for only three suspects, each of whom had offered a confession. Eleven other suspects were acquitted in the next three sessions of the court. At length, even the three convicted witches were reprieved by order of the governor and released from jail later in 1693. During the same year, all other pending actions issuing from the Salem trials were terminated by a general pardon. After 1693, there are no further records of legal action against witchcraft in Massachusetts Bay.

These, then, are the bare chronological outlines of perhaps the best-known episode in the history of witchcraft. . . .

Theological Context

The Salem proceedings were premised upon the assumption that the cries of the afflicted were indeed a collective responsibility. . . .

The belief that afflictions were a collective responsibility had its roots in what [historian] Perry Miller has called "the master idea" of the New England Puritans—the doctrine of the national covenant. Even before the actual habitation and settlement of the wilderness, the founders of New England conceived of the colony as bound by a special relationship to God. [First governor John] Winthrop articulated the terms of this relationship in midvoyage aboard the *Arbella:*

> Thus stands the cause between God and us, wee are entered into Covenant with him for this worke, wee have taken out a Commission, the Lord hath given us lease to draw our owne Articles we have professed to enterprise these Accions upon these and these ends, we have hereupon besought him of favor and blessing.

Within this covenantal framework, the Puritans accorded the colony a legitimacy that transcended royal prerogative. New England was not a mere commercial enterprise to be encouraged or discarded according to its material success.

As the current repository of God's truth, the destiny of the settlement was linked to a far grander imperative. The measure of New England was the success with which the community fulfilled its covenantal obligation to God. . . .

For a chosen people, the judgments of Providence were sure and exact. Crop failures, epidemics, Indian raids, and sundry other disasters were perceived not as accidents or as the mere logical concomitants of wilderness living but rather as judgments rendered according to the moral failings of the community. As the national sins increased, so would the severity of divine afflictions. Insofar as God maintained his covenant with New England, the members would have clear and continuous guidelines regarding the extent of their progress toward or departure from the realization of communal goals.

Crop failures, epidemics, Indian raids, and sundry other disasters were perceived . . . as judgments rendered according to the moral failings of the community.

Until the deeply troubled decade of the 1690s, there was little fear that these guidelines would disappear. No matter how grave the crisis and, by direct inference, no matter how far the community had degenerated, few civil and ecclesiastical leaders of the first two generations ever seriously doubted that the Puritan mission was salvageable.

For the first generation of ministers, the idea of the national covenant furnished not only a tool for diagnosing the ills of the society but a means for solving them as well. In response to the various judgments of war and calamity issued by an angry Providence, the General Court would order a day of humiliation in which members were enjoined to acknowledge their sins through prayer and fasting. Through such communal rituals, civil and ecclesiastical leaders sought not only to safeguard New England's covenantal status but to actively restore peace and prosperity.

The second generation of ministers broke with this formula. Gradually, the catalog of public misfortunes began to include not just external disasters but the sins and corruptions of the community itself. [Historian Perry] Miller gives

October 19, 1652, as the date when the General Court included for the first time the moral failings of New England—"the worldly-mindedness, oppression, and hardheartedness to be feared among us"—as well as the routine list of devastations as reasons for a public fast.

This emphasis upon spiritual corruption and moral deficiency reached its literary apotheosis between approximately 1660 and 1690 in a type of sermon that Miller has termed the jeremiad. The jeremiad imparted a new meaning to the misfortunes that befell New England. The disasters visited upon the community were viewed less as the occasion for collective propitiation than as the punishment for collective sin. . . .

By the early 1690s, ecclesiastical denunciation had escalated almost to the point where the success of a sermon could be measured by the vividness of its portrait of impending doom. It is in the context of this ever-expanding repertory of dire prophecies that the community was prepared for the most shocking demonstration of all. The judgment of witchcraft was the final realization of what ministers had been warning the members of for years. . . .

Colonial Status

If the jeremiad provided a ready vehicle for the expression of gloomy predictions, the events of the previous decade endowed these predictions with plausibility. At the time of the Salem trials, the future of the Puritan mission in America was in real jeopardy. The prospect of political dislocation within the British Empire, combined with involvement in a fierce and costly war with the French and their Indian allies, more than fulfilled the dire expectations of the ministers.

Particularly disruptive were the relations between the colony and the English government. In 1684, after having allowed colonial political autonomy for over fifty years, English authorities decided to exercise stronger controls. The charter of 1629—the document that legitimated the colonial right of self-government—was revoked by order of King Charles II. The immediate effect of this cancelation was to undermine the validity of colonial civil institutions.

Following Charles's death in 1685, his successor, King James II, appointed an official with authority to form his own advisory council in place of the General Court. The first of these appointees, Joseph Dudley, met with the General Court on May 17, 1686, to inform the members that their charter privileges had been terminated. Dudley's tenure as "President of the Territory and Dominion of New England" lasted only seven months, however. His successor, Sir Edmond Andros, a devout Anglican, arrived in Boston on December 20, 1686. Where Dudley had merely announced the dissolution of colonial institutions, the Andros regime proceeded as if the dissolution were already accomplished. Andros's refusal to recognize old land titles as well as his enactment of tax levies and other administrative changes without the consent of elected representatives incurred the opposition of the general public.

It may be that his insistence on holding Church of England services in one of the Boston meetinghouses produced the most provocative confrontation of all. When several Boston ministers protested against this desecration of one of their buildings, Andros seized the South Meetinghouse by force. Eventually, this proprietary dispute was resolved when a new site was found for the exclusive use of an Anglican congregation. Even this gesture did little to alleviate the conflict between Andros and the Boston clergy. Indeed, when a military excursion into Canada failed in 1690, several ministers attributed the disaster to God's anger at the infiltration of Anglicans among his chosen people.

The Salem trials coincided with a moment of grave uncertainty about the future of New England.

Finally, encouraged by the English revolt against King James II in 1688, the members of the Massachusetts Bay successfully deposed Andros and held him captive while several members of his council were imprisoned. With the accession of William and Mary to the throne of England, indigenous civil and ecclesiastical institutions were revived, albeit only provisionally. A temporary governing authority, headed by Simon Bradstreet, presided over the Massachusetts Bay for the next three years. During his administration, Bradstreet resurrected the General Court and petitioned the crown for the continuance of the original charter.

Not until October 1691 was political and institutional stability restored through the ratification of a new charter, which formally recognized Massachusetts Bay as a province within the British Empire. The price of this stability, however, was to place the Puritan mission in further jeopardy, for the charter of 1691 required that the political boundaries of Massachusetts be reconstituted to include previously disenfranchised religious groups. The effect of this provision was to open the channels of political power to groups such as Quakers and Anglicans, for whom the New England experiment was anathema. The problem of how to maintain Puritan hegemony without contravening this provision for a dangerously enlarged franchise would plague civil and ecclesiastical authorities throughout the first half of the eighteenth century.

Threat of Attack

During the same period, Massachusetts Bay faced yet another challenge to its existence. In the intensification of the French and Indian War between 1689 and 1697, the colonists of New England learned to perceive the wilderness less as a force to be mastered in accordance with divine plan than as a menacing presence that threatened to encroach on their territories. The God who had delivered the inhabitants through successful campaigns against the Indians in the 1670s now imposed upon his people a more alarming trial. In the unsuccessful invasion of Quebec in 1690, the members were warned that a wrathful and angry God might even permit his chosen people to fail.

In the early 1690s, virtually no colonial border was safe from attack. In January 1691, one town on the northern periphery between New Hampshire and Maine was successfully attacked, and close to a hundred members of the community were killed. Later military excursions in July and August into Lancaster, Brookfield, and Billerica brought home to the settlers of Massachusetts the precariousness of their own borders. . . .

A Context of Social Upheaval

The Salem trials coincided with a moment of grave uncertainty about the future of New England. The course charted by the first generation had become less a guide to the destiny of God's chosen people than a disturbing reminder of how far the later generations had fallen. It was not merely that the prospect of a community of saints had not yet been realized. Far more troubling was the suspicion that the whole framework of the national covenant no longer applied to the New England experience.

For some members, the political reversals of Massachusetts Bay could only be a source of comfort. For Quakers, Anglicans, and other dissident sects, the collapse of Puritan theocracy promised an end to religious persecution. For others, who viewed New England in terms of its economic possibilities, the weakening of ecclesiastical controls might even yield expanded opportunities for business and commerce. For those civil and ecclesiastical leaders who identified with the goals of the founders, however, the abandonment of the national covenant signified nothing less than the loss of community. For ministers such as Cotton Mather and his father, a New England divested of its covenantal obligations to God was a New England beyond contemplation. For such men, the giving up of the Puritan mission yielded not social change but social extinction.

From an orthodox perspective, Massachusetts Bay, just before the Salem trials, presented the spectacle of a society at the point of dissolution. Already in 1689, Cotton Mather had remarked on the suicidal tendencies among his people: "Tis almost unaccountable, that at some time in some places here, melancholy distempered Ragings towards Self-Murder, have been in a manner, Epidemical." Early in 1692, large numbers of young persons had shocked the older generation by profaning the Sabbath. During the same period, in response to an increase in urban crime, Boston had been obliged to provide for the nocturnal security of its inhabitants. The aged merchant Joshua Scottow may well have articulated the ambience of the province when, in the early 1690s, he urged that a history be drawn up immediately because "how near New England now is to its breaking, the all-knowing One only knows."

It is in the context of this profound social upheaval that members began to discern the conspiracy of Satan against God's chosen people. For at least some of the clergy and magistrates, the discovery of witchcraft would offer not only an explanation for the impending collapse of the old order but, even more importantly, a final vindication of the Puritan mission in New England.

Factional Politics Provoked the Crisis in Salem Village

Bryan F. LeBeau

Creighton University professor Bryan F. LeBeau contends in this selection from *The Story of the Salem Witch Trials* that warring factions within Salem Village, which became polarized during the ministry of Reverend Samuel Parris, help explain why the witchcraft crisis occurred. According to LeBeau, the Salem Village factions were led by two families: the Porters, who maintained close commercial ties to nearby Salem Town and who wished to remain members of the Salem Town church, and the Putnams, whose livelihood came exclusively from farming and who supported Salem Village autonomy from Salem Town and a separate Salem Village church. The issue of Reverend Parris's parsonage and salary polarized the factions. The Putnams supported Parris and the Porters challenged him.

LeBeau claims that the 1692 crisis makes more sense when one considers that the first four afflicted girls were either members of the Putnam family, whose prosperity was diminishing, or the Parris family, whose security was in jeopardy. LeBeau points out that adult members of the Putnam family testified against thirty-nine accused witches; he considers factional politics a primary contributing factor to the witchcraft accusations.

Exactly why the witch-hunt of 1692 began in Salem village and not elsewhere in New England will perhaps

Excerpted from *The Story of the Salem Witch Trials*, by Bryan F. LeBeau (Upper Saddle River, NJ: Prentice-Hall, Inc., 1998). Copyright © 1998 by Prentice-Hall, Inc. Reprinted with permission.

never be fully explained. Historians of the Great European Witch-hunt, who have raised the question relative to other communities, have tended to focus on extraordinary strains with which those communities, for whatever reasons, were not able to cope. And to be sure, many New England communities had their fair share of strains. Several suffered from the economic, social, political, and religious dislocations of the modernization process of the Early Modern Period, but to a greater extent than others Salem village fell victim to warring factions, misguided leadership, and geographical limitations that precluded its dealing effectively with those problems.

Salem Village vs. Salem Town

In 1692, Salem village, now Danvers, had a population of about 600. It remained part of Salem town, but it had already earned the reputation of being one of New England's most contentious communities. Not surprisingly, when accusations of witchcraft were made, they followed the lines formed by that contentiousness. . . .

In 1692, Salem village . . . had already earned the reputation of being one of New England's most contentious communities.

Salem town allowed villagers to use their church tax to construct a meetinghouse of their own and to hire a minister. It did not authorize them, however, to establish an entirely separate congregation; thus, the minister of the village church could not distribute communion, baptize believers, or discipline its members, and those who attended retained their official membership elsewhere, mostly in the town church. Otherwise, villagers continued to pay all other town taxes; to have their constables and representatives to the General Court chosen by all town residents; and to have the town selectmen continue to set the prices at which their farm products could be sold, as well as to determine the location of new roads and the distribution of yet undistributed lands.

Acting on what limited autonomy they had been granted, Salem village residents met on November 11, 1672, to elect a committee to plan the construction of their new church and to hire their first minister. Accomplishing both, however, did little to ease strained relations between the village and Salem town. Moreover, it exacerbated a growing rift within the village itself, between those who sought further independence from the town and those who opposed it. The establishment of a fully covenanted church and appointment of a like-minded minister became central to that quarrel.

Porters vs. Putnams

Kinship was a primary determinant of social action in the seventeenth-century Puritan New England community, so it is not surprising that the contending Salem village factions were led by two dominant families, the Porters and the Putnams. The patriarchs of both families had arrived in Salem in the 1640s, and through marriage, business, and politics gathered around them an extensive network of family, partners, and allies. The second generation had grown wealthy, but the Porters, who owned land primarily on the east side of the village and maintained close commercial ties to the town, grew more prosperous. By 1681, the three Putnam brothers—Thomas Sr., Nathaniel, and John Sr.—whose lands lay primarily in the northwestern part of the village, paid the largest taxes in the village. When lands outside of the village were included, however, the Porters paid even more.

Further, the Putnams, who relied almost exclusively on farming, faced a less-certain future. Not only did their land lack convenient access to markets by either land or water, but it was less arable, consisting in large part of hills and swampy meadows. Moreover, while the overall total of Putnam lands increased only slightly, it was being divided among a larger number of households. What was once distributed among three male Putnams, by the 1690s was being divided eleven ways.

The families' political fortunes diverged as well. The Porters excelled in town politics, the Putnams in village affairs. As early as 1646, John Porter was elected to the first of many terms as a Salem town selectman. In 1668, he served as deputy to the General Court. In 1661, he became a deacon in the Salem town church and upon his death in 1676 left it a bequest. The second generation followed their father's example, the most prominent being Israel Porter, who from 1679 through the end of the century served almost uninterruptedly as a town selectman.

Before 1672, the year the village church was established, the Putnams had been active in town affairs, even serving in town office. But thereafter, perhaps at first by choice but then almost certainly because of the rise to power of the town's commercial class, they focused almost exclusively on village affairs. From 1665 to 1673, for example, Nathaniel and John Putnam served a total of seven terms as town selectmen; for the next nineteen years, they served only five terms, and none of their sons took their places.

The one notable exception to this family pattern was Joseph, the second son and only child of Thomas Putnam Sr., by his second wife Mary. Upon Thomas's death in 1686, he left to Mary and, upon his maturity, to Joseph, the larger part of his estate, including the family homestead. Joseph's step-siblings were by no means excluded from their father's will. Thomas Jr. and Edward were given farms of their own, but they were convinced that their father had favored the son of his old age and second love. In 1690, Joseph Putnam, by then the wealthiest of all of the third-generation Putnams, married Elizabeth Porter, entering into an alliance with his family's enemies to which he remained faithful to the end.

Reverend Samuel Parris

Between 1672 and 1689, Salem village hired and then hounded out of office three ministers: James Bayley, George Burroughs, and Deodat Lawson. . . .

Finally there was Samuel Parris. Born in London in 1653, Parris moved with his family to Barbados, where his father became a sugar planter and merchant. He attended Harvard College, but in 1678, upon his father's death, he returned to the island, without his degree, as executor of his father's estate. He too became a merchant, but after about eight years, when his business was irreparably harmed by a devastating hurricane and a sustained drop in world sugar prices, Parris sold out and moved to Boston. He tried to compete with the city's already established men of commerce, but failing at that he opted for the ministry, and in November 1688, he preached for the first time in Salem village.

Upon his first visit Parris so sufficiently impressed the congregation that they voted to accept him as their minister, but it took months of protracted discussion over salary to complete the hiring process, as well as to sow the seeds of future discontent. On June 18, 1689, Parris's contract was recorded in the Village Book of Record, but negotiations over compensation continued. In October, the village committee—consisting of Nathaniel and John Putnam, Jonathan Walcott and Thomas Flint (both connected to the Putnams by marriage), and Nathaniel Ingersoll—voted to grant Parris the deed to the village parsonage and two acres of land. In 1681, the property had been set aside for the support of the village's minister, with the provision that it not be given to him, but the committee voted to rescind the earlier action. It may have been legal, but the decision was not universally popular. . . .

Of the first four afflicted girls in Salem village, two lived in the Samuel Parris household.

On October 16, 1691, members of the Porter faction—Joseph Porter, Joseph Hutchinson, Joseph Putnam, Daniel Andrew, and Francis Nurse—were elected to a majority of the village committee. Once in office, they promptly challenged the legality of Parris's ownership of the parsonage, and two months later they refused to assess taxes for the payment of Parris's 1692 salary. The Reverend Parris was in trouble, and he knew it. He announced from the pulpit that although through him Christ had "begun a new work" in Salem village, it was "the main drift of the Devil to pull it all down."

It was not a new message for the Reverend Parris; it had evolved over the past two years in response to the growing challenge to his ministry. As early as January 1690, he had warned his congregation that although they may have pretended to be friends, the "rotten-hearted" were neither to be trusted nor expected to keep their distance. They could infiltrate even innocent communities, a point he returned to in February when he warned that there was "great guiltiness upon this account in this poor little village," and again in January 1692, when he charged that a "great hatred ariseth even from nearest relations." In such sermons, Parris exacerbated the growing fear of one segment of his congregation of "outsiders," those of Salem town, but he also emphasized, to an even greater extent by 1692, the threat of internal subversion posed by those in their midst who were linked to those outsiders. . . .

Faction Provokes Crisis

By 1692, Salem village had reached the point of institutional, demographic, and economic polarization. The church served as the locus of one faction, the village committee served the other. Seventy percent of village church members supported the Reverend Parris, while only 13 percent opposed him. Of those who retained their membership in the town or other churches while worshipping in Salem village, only 56 percent supported Parris, almost all of the rest being listed among the opposition. Of the twelve wealthiest men of Salem village who made their opinions known, only four, all Putnams, supported Parris; eight, all Porters, opposed him. In contrast, of forty-six largely middle-class male residents whose positions were known, thirty-one backed Parris, while fifteen stood opposed. As [historians Paul] Boyer and [Stephen] Nissenbaum have concluded, Parris's opposition constituted a minority in the village, but they owned as much property as his more numerous supporters.

In geographic terms, Parris's opposition tended to come from those living on village lands nearest Salem town, especially along Ipswich Road, which connected the town to Boston. In that area, opponents outnumbered supporters by a ratio of six-to-one. Among residents of the northwestern half of the village, Parris's supporters led opponents four-to-one. In between lay an area in which proponents and opponents were more evenly divided, with an edge to Parris.

Under such circumstances, that the witch-hunt of 1692 began at Salem makes more sense than it does at first glance. Historic frustrations had been translated into a life-and-death struggle over a way of life. Of the first four afflicted girls in Salem village, two lived in the Samuel Parris household and a third was Ann Putnam, daughter of Thomas Putnam Jr.; three of the afflicted girls who lived in the household of Thomas Putnam Jr. formally testified against at least twenty-five accused witches; and those same three girls were backed by adult members of the Putnam clan, seven of whom testified or signed complaints against thirty-nine of the accused witches, which could be no coincidence.

We should recall, however, a point made at the outset: the people of seventeenth-century Salem believed in witches. Further, there is no direct evidence by which we can attribute those charges brought in the Salem witch trials entirely to factional politics or to a conscious effort on the part of one group to punish the other for economic and political wrongs. But in the end, even the young girls could not have been oblivious to the bitterness and resentment that had pervaded their own household. When leaders of the pro-Parris faction, including Parris himself, resorted to denouncing their opponents as morally defective individuals—demonizing them, if you will—it was only one small step further to attribute their behavior to the influence of the Devil.

3

The Salem Witch-Hunt Was Driven by a Conspiracy

Enders A. Robinson

In the sixty years prior to 1692 about one hundred people were formally indicted for witchcraft in New England, and of the twenty convicted, sixteen were executed. The Salem witch crisis differs from earlier New England witch scares in the sheer volume of accusations made within a very short period of time. In less than one year nearly two hundred were accused and nineteen executed. The number of accusations has led some interpreters of the event to consider the Salem witch-hunt a product of mass hysteria. Enders A. Robinson, however, argues that the initial seventy-four accusations were the work of a core group of conspirators.

In this excerpt from his book, *The Devil Discovered: Salem Witchcraft 1692*, Robinson tabulates information from extant official documents to reveal the identities of the conspirators. He then speculates about their probable reasons for testifying against their neighbors.

Social and political conditions courted disaster in Salem Village. Friction between two rival factions, exacerbated by the inflammatory rhetoric of Reverend Samuel Parris, sparked a witch hunt. Yet the normal checks and balances in the New England community should have limited its growth and brought it to a speedy end. In the case of Salem witchcraft, quite the opposite happened. The witch hunt

Excerpted from *The Devil Discovered: Salem Witchcraft 1692*, by Enders A. Robinson (New York: Hippocrene Books, 1991). Copyright © 1991 by Enders A. Robinson. Reprinted with permission.

spread easily and rapidly. The entire system of New England justice under law seemed to collapse.

Many reasons have been advanced to explain why the Salem witch hunt was transformed from a brushfire into a firestorm. Was the Salem witch hunt a product of mass hysteria, and was it fueled by growing numbers of accusations of neighbor against neighbor? Did it spread like a fire out of control, indiscriminately burning all in its path, rich and poor alike? Or was the firestorm ignited by a small group of men? Did one tightly-knit conspiracy provide the accusations? . . .

Most of the legal complaints drawn up in 1692 are extant today, the names of the accusers boldly standing forth. If the accusers represented a random sample of the general

Complaint Table©

Date	Accused	Accusers	Afflicted
No. 1 Feb. 29	Sarah Good Sarah Osborne Tituba	Thomas Putnam Edward Putnam Joseph Hutchinson Thomas Preston	Elizabeth Parris Abigail Williams Ann Putnam, Jr. Elizabeth Hubbard
No. 2 Mar. 19	Martha Corey	Edward Putnam Henry Kenny	Abigail Williams Ann Putnam, Sr. Ann Putnam, Jr. Mercy Lewis Elizabeth Hubbard
No. 3 Mar. 23	Rebecca Nurse	Edward Putnam Jonathan Putnam	Abigail Williams Ann Putnam, Jr.
No. 4 Mar. 23	Dorcas Good	Edward Putnam Jonathan Putnam	Ann Putnam, Jr. Mary Walcott Mercy Lewis
No. 5 Mar. 29	Rachel Clinton	Complaint (filed at Ipswich) not extant	Not extant
No. 6 Apr. 4	Sarah Cloyce Elizabeth Proctor	Jonathan Walcott Nathaniel Ingersoll	Abigail Williams John Indian Mary Walcott Ann Putnam, Jr. Mercy Lewis
No. 7 Apr. 11	John Proctor	No formal complaint. Arrested at his wife's examination (above).	Same as for his wife

public, then it can be concluded that the witch hunt was caused by mass hysteria. However, if the accusers were members of a small interlocked group, then it can be concluded that this group formed a conspiracy. The question of whether the witch hunt was driven by mass hysteria or by conspiracy can be answered by simply tabulating all the legal complaints filed with the official documents. . . .

The Case for Conspiracy

Even a cursory study of the preceding table reveals a hard core of accusers belonging to the extended family of Thomas Putnam. Besides Thomas Putnam there were his brother Edward Putnam, his brother-in-law Jonathan Walcott, his uncle-in-law Nathaniel Ingersoll, his uncles John Putnam, Sr. and Nathaniel Putnam, and his first cousins Jonathan Putnam and John Putnam, Jr. These men formed the Putnam contingent of a conspiracy.

Thomas Putnam exerted complete control over the actions of the two afflicted girls living in his household, his eldest daughter, Ann Putnam, Jr., age twelve, and his servant Mercy Lewis, age seventeen.

Jonathan Walcott had similar authority over another of the afflicted girls, his daughter Mary Walcott, age seventeen. Mary's natural mother was dead, and her step-mother was Thomas Putnam's sister, Deliverance (Putnam) Walcott. Mary's great uncle was Nathaniel Ingersoll.

The afflicted girls also include Elizabeth Parris, age nine, and Abigail Williams, age eleven. Elizabeth, called Betty, was the daughter of the Rev. Samuel Parris; Abigail, called Nabby, was his niece who also lived in his household. The Rev. Samuel Parris, a strict disciplinarian, would not have allowed their participation without his tacit approval.

The name of Elizabeth Hubbard, age seventeen, also appears among the afflicted girls. She was the great niece of the wife of Dr. William Griggs. Working as a servant in his household Elizabeth, by necessity, took her cues from him.

Whenever we see the names of either Elizabeth Parris or Abigail Williams on a complaint, we know that the Rev. Parris was involved. Whenever we see the name Elizabeth Hubbard, we know that Dr. Griggs was involved. These men never would have permitted such exploitation otherwise. It follows that Parris and Griggs were also members of the conspiracy, making up the professional contingent.

Why, then, did the Rev. Samuel Parris and Dr. William Griggs not sign their names on the complaints? As minister and doctor, they occupied the two highest professional positions in the community, guarding the spiritual and physical health of those entrusted to them. To become involved with the actual legal mechanics of a witch hunt would have been unseemly. Yet one is tempted to say that they signed the complaints with invisible ink. . . .

The Conspirators' Motivations

Sergeant Thomas Putnam, age thirty-nine, a founding member of the conspiracy, acted as ringleader. Much can be learned by looking at events from the perspective of this man, the chief filer of the legal complaints that led to the arrest of alleged witches. Repeatedly he claimed that his eldest daughter, Ann Putnam, Jr., and his servant Mercy Lewis were afflicted and tormented by a multitude of witches. He demanded justice.

His wife Ann Putnam, Sr., age thirty, entered into this macabre play-act as an afflicted person on a number of occasions. In fact she was in court almost as often as her daughter and her servant, all of them acting out the afflictions of witchcraft. Together, the three were responsible for the spectral evidence leading to many imprisonments, some of which resulted in death.

[There was] a hard core of accusers belonging to the extended family of Thomas Putnam. . . . These men formed the Putnam contingent of a conspiracy.

Mother Ann and daughter Ann were a particularly formidable pair of actors. People from miles around trooped into the courtroom to watch their performances under bewitchment. They regarded their afflictions as a matter of life and death. During the course of the witch hunt, Ann Putnam, Jr. alleged that she was afflicted by a total of sixty-two persons. She testified against many people in court, and gave a number of affidavits.

In 1692 Mercy Lewis was a well-educated young woman. She was born in 1675, the daughter of Philip Lewis of Casco, Maine. . . .

When Mercy Lewis' parents were both killed by the Indians in 1689, she was taken into the house of the Rev. Burroughs. In 1690, as the only minister for all the towns between Casco and Wells, Maine, he took up residency in Wells. Because of the danger of repeated Indian attacks in Maine, Mercy was placed in the home of William and Rachel Bradford. Mercy lived a part of a year with them, during which they did "judge in the matter of conscience of speaking the truth and untruth, she would stand stiffly [original document torn]." She was finally placed as a servant in the home of Sergeant Thomas Putnam in Salem Village. . . .

Sergeant Thomas Putnam's brother, Deacon Edward Putnam, age thirty-eight in 1692, was a member of the conspiracy and his closest ally in carrying out the witch hunt.

When it was formed in February 1692, the nascent conspiracy never could have guessed the extremes to which they would be allowed to go.

Another member, Captain Jonathan Walcott, was the father of Mary Walcott by his first wife. At the time of the witch hunt, he was fifty-two, and married to his second wife, Deliverance, the sister of Thomas and Edward Putnam. Not only did Captain Walcott encourage his daughter Mary Walcott to act out the role of an afflicted girl, but he testified with great effectiveness against many accused witches himself.

Records show that Mary Walcott alleged that she was afflicted by fifty-nine persons. She gave many affidavits and frequently testified in court against people. Mary Walcott and Ann Putnam, Jr. were taken to Andover on June 11, 1692, to initiate a witch hunt in that area. Again, on July 26, the two girls visited that town to spur on the Andover witch hunt. . . .

Sergeant Thomas Putnam's two uncles John Putnam, Sr. and Nathaniel Putnam were eager to help. They were members of the conspiracy, but were not as active as the younger Putnams.

John Putnam, Sr. had married Rebecca Prince, stepdaughter of John Gedney, Sr., the wealthy owner of the Ship Tavern in Salem Town. In 1692 John Putnam, Sr. believed that his nephews, the two Prince boys, were being cheated out of their inheritance by Sarah Osborne. To destroy Sarah Osborne, John Putnam, Sr. saw to it that she was one of the first three witches accused. Sarah Osborne died in prison a couple of months later. John Putnam, Sr. also took his revenge on the Rev. George Burroughs by testifying against him in the witchcraft trials. . . .

Lieutenant Nathaniel Ingersoll, the innkeeper, was the final member of the conspiracy. He was the uncle of Captain Jonathan Walcott. Lieutenant Ingersoll worked closely with Sergeant Thomas Putnam and Captain Walcott to keep the flames burning. With a wary eye toward maintaining goodwill so as not to impair the profits of his tavern, Ingersoll signed only a few complaints. However, when called as witness he gladly testified against those accused. It was no coincidence that two of his competitors in Salem Village, tavern-owners John Proctor and Edward Bishop, Jr. were both arrested for witchcraft, and that Proctor paid with his life. . . .

When it was formed in February 1692, the nascent conspiracy never could have guessed the extremes to which they would be allowed to go. Its members suspected that vindictive people in Salem Village and neighboring communities would support their cause of rooting out certain undesirable people as witches. They trusted that the powerful personage, John Hathorne, who gave original encouragement would continue in his support. What they could not foresee, however, was that the highest level of government, the ruling, old-guard Puritans, would not only act in collusion to support their cause of destroying the "enemies of the church," but would give them a free hand in determining who those enemies were.

4

Devilish Hypocrites in the Church

Samuel Parris

The sermon Reverend Samuel Parris delivered on March 27, 1692, "Christ Knows How Many Devils There Are," has been identified by University of Missouri professor of history Larry Gragg as pivotal in the progress of the Salem witch crisis. In the sermon Reverend Parris uses Judas as an example of devilish hypocrites who can be found among church members. The idea that devils sit with saints in church contributed to the suspicion and fear which issued in more accusations against respectable church members in Salem Village during the spring of 1692.

O ccasioned by dreadful Witchcraft broke out here a few weeks past, and one Member of this Church, and another of Salem, upon public examination by Civil Authority vehemently suspected for she-witches, and upon it committed.

John 6: 70. "Have not I chosen you twelve, and one of you is a Devil." . . .

Doctrine: *Our Lord Jesus Christ knows how many Devils there are in his Church, and who they are.*

1. There are devils as well as saints in Christ's Church.
2. Christ knows how many of these devils there are.
3. Christ knows who these devils are.

Proposition 1: There are devils as well as saints in Christ's church. Here three things may be spoken to: (1) Show you what is meant here by *devils;* (2) That there are

Excerpted from Samuel Parris's sermon before Salem Village, March 27, 1692.

such devils in the church; (3) That there are also true saints in such churches.

(1). What is meant here by *devils?* "One of you is a devil." Answer: By *devil* is ordinarily meant any wicked angel or spirit. Sometimes it is put for the prince or head of the evil spirits, or fallen angels. Sometimes it is used for vile and wicked persons—the worst of such, who for their villainy and impiety do most resemble devils and wicked spirits. Thus Christ in our text calls Judas a devil: for his great likeness to the devil. "One of you is a devil": i.e., a devil for quality and disposition, not a devil for nature—for he was a man, etc.—but a devil for likeness and operation (John 8: 38, 41, 44—"Ye are of your father the devil.")

(2). There are such devils in the church. Not only sinners, but notorious sinners; sinners more like to the devil than others. So here in Christ's little Church. (Text.) This also Christ teacheth us in the parable of the tares (Matth. 13: 38), where Christ tells us that such are the children of the wicked one—i.e., of the devil. Reason: Because hypocrites are the very worst of men—*corruptio optimi est pessima* [corrupted best and worst]. Hypocrites are the sons and heirs of the devil, the free-holders of hell—whereas other sinners are but tenants. When Satan repossesseth a soul, he becomes more vile and sinful (Luke 11: 24–26). As the jailer lays loads of iron on him that hath escaped. None are worse than those who have been good, and are naught; and might be good, but will be naught.

(3). There are also true saints in the church. The church consists of good and bad: as a garden that has weeds as well as flowers, and as a field that has wheat as well as tares. Hence that gospel is compared to a net that taketh good and bad (Matth. 13: 47–50). Here are good men to be found— yea, the very best; and here are bad men to be found—yea, the very worst. Such as shall have the highest seat in glory, and such also as shall be cast into the lowest and fiercest flames of misery. Saints and devils, like Jeremiah's basket of figs (Jer. 24: 1–4).

Proposition 2: Christ knows how many of these devils there are in his churches. As in our text there was one among the twelve. And so in our churches God knows how many devils there are: whether one, two, three, or four in twelve—how many devils, how many saints. He that knows whom he has chosen (John 13: 18), he also knows who they

are that have not chosen him, but prefer farms and mer-
chandise above him and above his ordinances (2 Tim. 4: 10).

Proposition 3: Christ knows who these devils are. There
is one among you, says Christ to the twelve: Well, who is
that? Why, it is Judas. Why, so Christ knows how many
devils among us—whether one, or ten, or twenty; and also
who they are. He knows us perfectly; and he knows those of
us that are in his church, that we are either saints or devils,
true believers or hypocrites and dissembling Judases that
would sell Christ and his kingdom to gratify a lust. We do
not think we are such (II Kings 8: 12–13).

5

Reverend Samuel Parris Triggered the Witch-Hunt

Larry Gragg

In the early months of 1692, the Salem Village pastor, Samuel Parris, was in danger of losing his job. The newly elected members of the village council had refused to assess taxes for his 1692 salary, and Reverend Parris felt his ministry was being subverted by devilish forces. Then in mid-February 1692, Parris's daughter and his niece began to exhibit such alarming behaviors that his home also seemed to be afflicted by the forces of evil. In this selection from his critical biography of Samuel Parris, *A Quest for Security*, Larry Gragg contends that Reverend Parris's reactions to the children's frightening afflictions "helped trigger the largest witch-hunt in American history." Parris created an atmosphere of crisis by convening large group prayers and fasts instead of isolating the afflicted girls, Gragg explains; furthermore, Parris fueled the fear and suspicion of his congregation by preaching in late March 1692 that prosperous members of the church, not just derelicts and outcasts, could be witches also. A dramatic increase in the number of people accused of being witches followed Parris's sermon.

As Samuel Parris fretted about the general assault of Satan's forces on the Church in late January and early February 1692, he faced a more vexing, personal crisis. Unbeknownst to him, his daughter, Elizabeth, and niece, Abigail Williams, along with other New England youth [as Boston minister Cotton Mather phrased it], "had been led away with little Sorceries." Although it is not precisely clear what Betty

From *A Quest for Security: The Life of Samuel Parris, 1653–1720*, by Larry Gragg (Westport, CT: Greenwood Press, 1990). Copyright © 1990 by Larry Gragg. Reprinted by permission of Greenwood Publishing Group, Inc.

and Abigail were doing, the available evidence suggests that they were experimenting with techniques of fortune-telling. John Hale, the pastor at the nearby Beverly church, explained in an account of the witchcraft episode published in 1702, that a number of young people "through a vain curiosity to know their future condition, have tampered with the Devil's tools." Specifically, Hale had heard about one girl who had tried "with an egg and a glass to find her future husband's calling, till there came up a coffin, that is, a specter in likeness of a coffin." Hale's account essentially squares with the testimony of Sarah Cole of Lynn, Massachusetts, who later in the year was accused of witchcraft. Cole admitted "that she & some others toyed w'th a Venus glase & an Egg. What trade their sweet harts should be of." Whatever the girls in the Parris home were doing, they had begun to act strangely as a result. Their "afflictions" both puzzled and frightened the minister, and his subsequent reactions helped trigger the largest witch hunt in American History.

Parris Appeals to Religious and Medical Experts

The afflictions suffered by the girls obviously shocked those who observed them. The girls fell into fits, former Salem Village pastor Deodat Lawson explained, "so strange as a well person could not Screw their Body into." The violence of their movements was "much beyond the Ordinary force" of the girls when they were in "their right mind." The Reverend John Hale offered a more graphic account of the afflictions. "These Children," he wrote, "were bitten and pinched by invisible agents; their arms, necks, and backs turned this way and that way, and returned back again, so it was impossible for them to do of themselves." As Lawson had done, Hale ruled out any natural cause for the alarming behavior. The convulsions were "beyond the power of any Epileptick Fits, or natural Disease to effect." Clearly, Hale had witnessed the girls' suffering, "Sometimes they were taken dumb, their mouths stopped, their throats choked, their limbs wracked and tormented so as might move an heart of stone." Given the severity of their fits, it is not surprising that Parris consulted a number of physicians, in an effort to discover the cause of the girls' suffering. One of them must have been Dr. William Griggs who bought a house and nineteen acres in the village on February 19. His wife's niece, seventeen-year-old Elizabeth Hubbard, may also have been "afflicted" at this time. It is likely, then, that Griggs was the physician who offered the diagnosis that the girls in the Parris household "were under an Evil Hand." In other words, some person or persons, utilizing the powers of witchcraft, were harming the girls. . . .

The afflictions soon spread throughout the neighborhood. The families affected "applied themselves to Fasting and Prayer." Such an approach had worked in other cases, notably with the Goodwin children. As Cotton Mather had concluded, "Prayer and Faith was the thing which drove the Divels from the Children." Reverend Parris went a step further by calling upon "some Worthy Gentlemen of Salem, and some Neighbour Ministers to consult together at his House." The assembled dignitaries closely observed the afflicted and concurred that "the hand of Satan was in them." Yet, they offered Parris little that was helpful. His visitors advised him simply to [in the words of pastor John Hale] "sit still and wait upon the Providence of God to see what time might discover; and to be much in prayer for the discovery of what was yet secret."

Villagers Take Action

Mary Sibley, an aunt of one of the afflicted girls, Mary Walcott, meanwhile had taken more direct action. On February 25, she convinced Parris's two slaves, Tituba and John Indian, to try some counter-magic. They took some urine from the afflicted girls, mixed it with rye meal, and baked it "to find out the Witch [as Hale phrases it]." This occult experiment had unfortunate consequences for Tituba; the girls named her as their tormentor. The clergymen visiting Parris questioned Tituba who confessed to making the witchcake. While the slave asserted that she was not a witch, she did say that "her Mistress in her own Country [Barbados] was a Witch, and had taught her some means to be used for the discovery of a Witch and for the prevention of being bewitched."

When four afflicted girls, Abigail Williams, Elizabeth Parris, Elizabeth Hubbard, and Ann Putnam, also "cryed out upon" Sarah Osborne and Sarah Good, claiming that the three women "or their Specters in their Shapes did grievously torment them," four villagers decided to take legal action. Joseph Hutchinson, Thomas Putnam, Edward

Putnam, and Thomas Preston filed formal complaints against the three women. Warrants were issued for their arrest and constables Joseph Herrick and George Locker brought them in for a March 1 "examination." In the process, constable Herrick also searched, unsuccessfully, for "Images and such like" in hopes of finding incriminating physical evidence. Salem magistrates John Hathorne and Jonathan Corwin came out to the village to conduct the questioning. . . .

The actions [Parris] took, and failed to take, proved to be crucial in creating an atmosphere of crisis.

Tituba's detailed confession had left many questions unanswered. She had alleged that there had been four witches and a man involved in harming the girls and that nine people from the village and Boston had made a pact with Satan. Only two, Good and Osborne, had been arrested. If villagers believed Parris's slave, and the crowded meetinghouse at her examination reveals at the least an intense interest in her confession, they assuredly wondered about the threat posed by the unidentified remaining witches.

In such disturbing circumstances early Americans looked to their pastors for guidance. As [historian] John Demos has written, "They were the experts, the leading tacticians, the mightiest warriors in supernatural combat." Samuel Parris's responses to what was happening were important to many in the village. The actions he took, and failed to take, proved to be crucial in creating an atmosphere of crisis, one in which a thoroughgoing witch hunt developed.

Parris Creates an Atmosphere of Crisis

On the first day of the examinations, Parris, obviously eager to know more about the subject, secured a copy of William Perkins's highly regarded *A Discourse of the Damned Art of Witchcraft* (1608). There was much in Perkins's treatise to suggest that Parris's congregation indeed faced a crisis. Tituba's claim that there were more witches, for example, gained credence in light of Perkins's assertion that if a witch "either voluntarily, or at his or her examination, or at his or her death" testified that another person was a witch, ample evidence existed to issue a warrant for the examination of the individual named. While he did not mount an immediate crusade to discover their identity, Parris's subsequent actions indicate his conviction that a growing witch conspiracy was afoot in Salem Village.

The minister's immediate concern was the continued suffering of the girls. He called a number of private fasts, including one on March 11, to which he invited neighboring clergymen "to join with him in keeping a Solemn day of Prayer at his own House." The afflicted girls present that day, though largely quiet, began to have fits after the prayers concluded. Abigail Williams in particular "would sometimes seem to be in a Convulsion Fit, her Limbs being twisted several ways, and very stiff, but presently her Fit would be over," [as Robert Calef explains].

Parris . . . not only had two of the more seriously afflicted in his household, but also had the responsibility for the spiritual condition of all in the congregation.

It was probably at about this time that the Boston clergyman Cotton Mather suggested that the girls be separated and treated like Martha Goodwin four years earlier. In that case Mather had taken the eldest afflicted Goodwin child into his home and "cured" her through prayer and fasting. Moreover, Mather would not reveal the names of anyone the afflicted children called out in their fits because, as he argued, "we should be tender in such Relations, lest we wrong the Reputation of the Innocent by stories not enough enquired into." Mather did not indicate to whom he made his offer, nor who rejected it, but most likely it was Parris who not only had two of the more seriously afflicted in his household, but also had the responsibility for the spiritual condition of all in the congregation.

Parris did not entirely reject the notion of isolated therapy for the afflicted because he sent his daughter to stay with Stephen Sewall in Salem in late March. Nine-year-old Elizabeth slowly recovered, though not without some recurrences of frightening visions. On March 25, she "related, that the great Black Man came to her, and told her, if she would be ruled by him, she should have whatsoever she desired, and go to a Golden City." Mrs. Sewall told Elizabeth that it had been the Devil who had approached her "and he was a Lyar from the Beginning, and bid her tell him so, if he came again: which she did," [according to Reverend Deodat Lawson].

Had the Salem Village pastor adopted Mather's approach of isolated therapy with all the girls (and by mid-March almost a dozen girls and women were having fits) he may well have prevented the spread of the afflictions. Instead, Parris convened group fasts and prayer sessions, giving the girls' behavior considerable exposure beyond their appearances at the examinations of the accused. Not only did more people "catch" their hysteria and hear the names of those allegedly harming them, but also those afflicted displayed their erratic behavior with uncharacteristic boldness. By the third Sunday in March, they were even interrupting worship services.

Parris Appeals to Deodat Lawson

As the sense of crisis deepened, Parris invited former pastor Deodat Lawson to the village. Upon his arrival, March 19, Lawson heard that magistrates Hathorne and Corwin had issued another arrest warrant; this time for Martha Corey. . . .

The following day, Sunday, Parris turned over the pulpit to his visiting colleague. Martha Corey, scheduled to be examined the next day, was in the meetinghouse as were many of the afflicted. What ensued clearly shocked Lawson and certainly the congregation which was accustomed to the dignified decorum of Sunday worship. Some of the girls had "Sore Fits" which interrupted Lawsons's opening prayer. Then, after the congregation sang a psalm, Abigail Williams demanded of him, "'Now stand up, and Name your Text': And after it was read, she said, 'It is a long Text.'" An afflicted woman, Ann Pope, also became an immediate and outspoken critic. As Lawson began his sermon, she said, "Now there is enough of that." Later in the sermon, Abigail Williams broke in with a reference to Martha Corey. She "called out, 'Look where Goodw. C sits on the Beam suckling her yellow bird betwixt her fingers'!" There were other disruptions. Twelve-year-old Ann Putnam said to those near her that she saw a yellow bird on Lawson's hat which was hanging on a pin on the pulpit. The frustrated preacher was interrupted again in his afternoon sermon. Abigail Williams, "upon my referring to my Doctrine said to me, 'I know no Doctrine you had, If you did name one, I had forgot it.'" Given a public forum, the afflicted, primarily Parris's niece, had further shocked the congregation and cast suspicions upon another woman.

The meetinghouse predictably was "Thronged with Spectators" on Monday to witness the Salem magistrates' examination of Martha Corey. . . .

Two days later Deodat Lawson visited twelve-year-old Ann Putnam's mother, Ann. She was one of the growing number of afflicted adults in the village. Weakened by an earlier fit, Ann Putnam was in bed when the minister arrived. As he prayed with her, she experienced another fit. After her husband Thomas helped her out of bed, the woman "began to strive violently with her Arms and Leggs." She also engaged in a debate with the "Apparition" of Rebecca Nurse who Putnam claimed afflicted her and tried to get her to sign the Devil's book. She recovered only after Lawson read the Scripture she had called out, "the third Chapter of the Revelations." This was the second time Lawson had heard accusations made against Rebecca, the elderly and respected wife of a prosperous village farmer, Francis Nurse. During his first evening in the village, Abigail Williams had called out her name during a fit.

The complaints prompted magistrates Corwin and Hathorne to issue a warrant for the old woman's arrest. . . .

The violent fits which convinced John Hathorne of Rebecca Nurse's guilt, more importantly frightened terribly the villagers in the meetinghouse. The assembly, Deodat Lawson wrote, "was struck with consternation, and they were afraid, that those that sate next to them, were under the influence of Witchcraft." Because of their terror, many villagers had become suspicious of virtually everyone. At this critical juncture the residents of Salem Village desperately wanted and received explanations of what was happening to them. . . .

Parris's Explanation and Impact on Subsequent Accusations

Parris offered clear-cut positions to his congregation. The most crucial concern he had to deal with was the possibility of a church member being a witch. Ever since accusations were made against Martha Corey, a growing number of people had openly wondered how a person they had assumed was one of God's elect could be in league with Satan. . . .

One of the more disturbing elements of Parris's sermon was his suggestion that there might be more witches in the Salem Village church.

From the announcement of his text, Samuel Parris's position . . . was clear. "Have not I chosen you twelve, & one of you is a Devil." Just as Christ knew there was a hypocrite among his apostles, Parris asserted that Puritans must realize that there were "Devils as well as Saints in the Church of Christ." The church had true saints and "Hypocrites & dissembling Judases" like Martha Corey and Rebecca Nurse. Hypocrites were the worst of sinners because they had permitted Satan to repossess their souls and when they did they became "more vile & sinfull." Church membership, Parris asserted, did not guarantee salvation. Some "Profess much love to Christ, but indeed are in league with their lusts." Such people "are Devils in Christs account." One of the more disturbing elements of Parris's sermon was his suggestion that there might be more witches in the Salem Village church than Martha Corey. "Christ knows how many Devils among us," he said, "whither one or ten or 20!" Just as those in the meetinghouse to observe Rebecca Nurse's examination had wondered if the person next to them was "under the influence of witchcraft," those who heard Samuel Parris must have wondered who else in the congregation was a devil and not a saint. . . .

Salem Village happened to have a minister who reacted in a particular way to the forces which he believed threatened both family and church. In calling in numerous medical and religious experts, and in largely rejecting isolation therapy, Parris not only gave wide exposure to the suffering of the afflicted, but also to the names they called out. Moreover, such an approach allowed those convinced that they were bewitched to reinforce each other's hysteria. By mid-March, the afflicted could even, according to Deodat Lawson, "foretel when another Fit was a-coming, and would say, 'Look to her she will have a Fit presently.'" Most importantly, Parris strenuously argued that church membership was no guarantee that a person was a saint of God. The church of "visible saints" the congregation had been attempting to build in the previous three years, in his judgment, included hypocrites and devils. The message was clear. Witches were not necessarily deviants, derelicts, or outcasts. Prosperous neighbors and professors of Christ might well be in league with Satan. In a real sense, everyone was suspect. . . .

The impact of Samuel Parris's response to the outbreak of witchcraft in Salem Village is evident in the dramatic increase in the number of accusations made by the afflicted: seven accusations in February and March; two dozen in April; and about twice that many in May. By summer's end, according to one account, "accusations were being made so freely and widely that accurate records of the official proceedings were no longer kept." At least 140 and perhaps as many as 200 faced the prospect of official interrogation.

6

Tituba's Testimony Exacerbated the Witch-Hunt

Elaine G. Breslaw

In this selection from her book, *Tituba, Reluctant Witch of Salem*, Elaine G. Breslaw argues that the testimony of Tituba, Reverend Parris's West Indian servant, "is the key to understanding why the events of 1692 took on such epic significance." Breslaw explains that Tituba confirmed the community's fear that the Devil was active in Salem by describing a witch meeting, a pact with an evil man, and a diabolical book with nine names in it. Breslaw believes that Tituba's testimony was intended to convince others of Reverend Parris's evil ways, but that it also revealed Tituba's resentment of people with high social status and her discontent with her state of servitude. Whatever Tituba's intentions may have been, the result of her testimony was a widening of the witch-hunt to include men, clergy, women of high social status, and strangers from other towns and cities.

O n the last day of February 1692, a leap year, Joseph Hutchinson, Edward and Thomas Putnam, and Thomas Preston appeared before Salem magistrates John Hathorne and Jonathan Corwin to make complaints against the three accused women for "suspition of Witchcraft." They charged that Sarah Osborne, Tituba, and Sarah Good had been using occult means to injure four girls over a period of two months. Four girls—Betty Parris, Abigail

Williams, Ann Putnam, and Elizabeth Hubbard, all under eighteen years of age—added their testimony to support the complaints. Thus began the legal process that focused attention on Tituba and would eventually lead to the imprisonment of more than one hundred people over a period of nine months and the execution of twenty between June 19 and September 22. A few more would die in prison from exposure and disease, adding a gruesome note to the death toll from this witch scare. Tituba would escape with her life, but she would spend thirteen months in a crowded, foul-smelling, and filthy Boston prison, unsure of her fate.

Tituba's . . . testimony confirmed the worst fears of a diabolical presence and gave the Salem worthies reason to launch a witchhunt.

Tituba's subsequent testimony confirmed the worst fears of a diabolical presence and gave the Salem worthies reason to launch a witchhunt. She supplied the essential legal evidence required to begin the process of communal exorcism, to purge the community of its collective sin. Without her testimony the trials could not have taken place. Thus it was only after Tituba began to confess that the witchhunt began in earnest. In her fantasies of an evil power, the Indian woman confirmed that the Devil was now among them. . . .

Tituba's Testimony

As is typical of witchcraft interrogation in all cultures, Tituba's questioners provided her with clues as to what her answers should be. Since those accused of witchcraft were usually innocent of the charges, such testimonies were more often an affirmation of the questioners' ideas about witchcraft than a revelation of the accused witches' particular beliefs and practices. A good part of Tituba's testimony was a direct response to those questions. She certainly understood some of what they wanted her to say and did give them the evidence needed to pursue their suspicions, but she also added details and notions that were not implied in the questions and set off a broader investigation than they had intended. Tituba's testimony was not merely the frightened response of a simple slave woman to the hints put forth by the magistrates, but an effective manipulation of their deepest fears. The impact of that confession triggered the witchhunt that defied all past experience with witchhunting in New England. In the process Tituba also led an assault on gender roles, social rank, and the clergy's authority, an attack that would be pursued relentlessly by the "afflicted" girls and the other confessors.

On the surface, in this cautious exchange between Tituba and her accusers, she seemed to ally herself with the Puritan theological notions of demonic evil, collaborating to assist in the process of purifying their society. But something more was at work. Hidden in that confession was not so much a Puritan concept of evil but one derived from non-Christian cultures; a set of ideas that was at once familiar and strange. The anomaly of this aberration heightened the fear of an invasive presence.

Covert Condemnation of Parris

When asked if she ever saw the Devil, Tituba acknowledged that "the devil came to me and bid me serve him." Who else did she see, asked the interrogator? Because she now knew he wanted others involved, Tituba answered, there were four women and a man. And who were they? Tituba identified two likely women who fit the popular image of a witch, Sarah Osborne and Sarah Good, both quarrelsome and somewhat disreputable, but already accused by the girls and thus understood by the magistrates as potential conspirators. The other three she did not know, but one was a tall man from Boston.

The man, according to Tituba's story, had visited her once before in late December or early January at the time that the children had first exhibited the bizarre symptoms. He appeared to her one night just as she was going to sleep. The Salem magistrates missed her cue. The dream was not even reported in the official record of her testimony taken by Ezekiel Cheever. It does appear in a more detailed report written by Jonathan Corwin. In Corwin's version she told them that the man-like shape came to her "Just as I was goeing to sleep . . . this was when the children was first hurt."

Tituba's nightmare of that evil presence may well have triggered memories of her earlier Barbados life, where dreams among both African and American Indians were thought to be the work of spirits and interpreted as omens of things to come. That ominous dream of an evil presence would be confirmed, in her mind, by the continuing illness of the children in the household and her own current misfortune to be identified with witchcraft. She sensed that Parris's wrath was the cause of Betty's problems, that the minister's continuing jeremiads against the ungrateful community and his terrifying warnings of future evils were taking their toll on the mental health of his daughter. By couching her accusation in the form of a sleep reference, in line with Indian beliefs in the identification of dreams as omens, she tried to inform others of Parris's evil ways. Her subversive suggestion was ignored.

Dreams were not significant elements in Puritan theology. They took her nightmare not as a visionary omen or spiritual experience but an actual occurrence that involved the specters of people they had to identify. Magistrates Hathorne and Corwin focused their questions on the activities of this odd group of creatures who inhabited the diabolical realm brought down to earth. "What is this appearance you see? . . . What did it say to you? . . . What did you say to it?" they asked.

A Witches' Meeting in Boston

Responding to their probing, Tituba embellished her story even more. The creatures all met in Boston at night where the five evil ones, including Sarah Good and Sarah Osborne, threatened her if she did not hurt the children. Tituba introduced a new element in witchcraft testimony, a witches' coven attended by the specters of people both known and unknown to her. The startled examiners paused to question her about this strange, distant meeting. Witchcraft accusations traditionally involved people known to each other, an aggrieved party usually could be suspected of causing harm to others. But Tituba told them that strangers were involved.

The interrogation of the other two accused women, Osborne and Good, had followed conventional tactics. In the face of continued denials, they had been asked in a prescribed sequence about the spirits they were familiar with, why they hurt the children or whom they used for that purpose, and finally about a covenant with the Devil. This procedure changed with the questioning of Tituba. The examiners did not immediately pursue the issue of a satanic pact.

They were distracted by her complex tale of an experience that took her from Boston back to Salem with orders to kill the children and of a specter that changed shape from that of a man to a dog and a hog. Joining this party of phantoms were a yellow bird, rats, a wolf and a cat, four women, and a hairy imp.

Veiled Indictment of the Wealthy

Additional details were elicited from Tituba on the dress and physical appearance of this group. Tituba specified that Osborne had a familiar with the head of a woman and two legs and wings similar to one previously described by Abigail. The tall man wore black clothes. One of the unidentified Boston women, Tituba said, wore a black hood over a white silk hood with a top knot. The other a shorter person had a serge coat and white cap. Tituba stated that she had seen the taller woman in Boston when she had lived there, but did not know her name. The silk clothing of the tall woman would indicate that Tituba had a person of higher class in mind; the shorter woman in wool and a white cap wore the dress of the more ordinary folk.

Sumptuary laws in Massachusetts prohibited men, women, and children from dressing in clothing made out of

Tituba told the magistrates that she had made a Satanic pact with a tall white man who claimed to be God and told her to hurt the children.

finer material. By order of October 14, 1651, the Massachu-setts General Court had forbidden people of "meane condi-tion" from wearing the "garbe of gentlemen" or women of the same rank from wearing "silke or tiffany hoodes or scar-fes, which though allowable to persons of greater estates, or more liberal education, yet, we cannot but judge it intollera-ble in persons of such like condition." The description of the woman in silk and the man in black were, therefore, veiled references to respectability and an attempt to identify mal-eficium with higher social status. The man's black clothing carried a connotation of dignity and formality. The silk worn by the "tall woman" denoted wealth.

When asked if she ever saw the Devil, Tituba acknowledged that "the devil came to me and bid me serve him."

Tituba's extraordinary message to her examiners was to look among the elite for the evil beings. That message, de-livered in a discrete and artful attack on the social class sys-tem, opened the way to the accusation of women of re-spectable sainthood, beginning with Martha Corey and Rebecca Nurse on March 19 and 23, respectively. The con-victions of these women would be eloquent testimony to the force of Tituba's suggestion that women eligible to wear silk could be witches. Her hints regarding the dangers hidden among the obviously respectable were confirmed and rein-forced by Parris's sermons later that month and by his early April warning that the Devil could lurk among the apparent saints. Her testimony confirmed the predictions of reform-ers who had reminded their congregations of an impending catastrophe if the community continued on its worldly path.

Hints of Clerical Misconduct

The strange, tall, white-haired man Tituba claimed to see wearing black clothes could fit many respectable, elderly men in the community dressed in their Sunday meeting clothes. In the imagination of some other confessed witches, obsessed by the rhetoric of race and in their fantasies of sa-tanic Indians, this tall Boston mystery man would be trans-formed into a tawny or black man. But he was clearly a white man in Tituba's recorded testimony, a devious reference to Samuel Parris, a clergyman with strong connections to Boston. In effect this part of her testimony triggered a search for an appropriate male scapegoat. The result was a widening of the witchhunt to include men; the arrest, conviction, and execution of several men; and the hanging of one clergyman, George Burroughs.

Whatever her intent, the consequence of Tituba's accusation in this community where words were believed to have the force of action, was to challenge the principle of social rank and raise the possibility of clerical misconduct. No one would be more likely to resent the special privilege of that class than a slave in the house of a Congregational minister. But Tituba's rudimentary anti-clericalism probably did not exist in isolation. She spoke to resentments against the special privilege and influence of the clergy harbored by other ordinary people, particularly young women. They would give vent to their hostility in later testimonies and confessions as they adapted and reformulated Tituba's stories to fit their own situations. Thus others, sensing the possible subversive message of a respectable white man leading a witch's coven, transformed Tituba's suggestion of an evil stranger into a parody of their own church rites—an indirect attack on the congregational ideal.

A Nightmarish Story

Questioned further about this strange group of people, Tituba said that they all met in Boston the night before. And how had they traveled there? Tituba described the ride through the night on "stickes," with Osborne and Good behind her. The man had appeared to her earlier that same evening while she was washing the lean-to room. This, she acknowledged, was her second encounter with the diabolical creature; he was the same one who appeared two months before in her dream.

The nightmarish story continued. Sometime during the morning of February 29, she was forced to pinch Elizabeth Hubbard at Dr. Grigg's house, where "the man brought her to me and made me pinch her." She regretted causing the child pain but could not stop doing so because they, "pull mee & hall me to . . . pinch the childr, & I am very sorry for itt." That night, Tituba testified, Good and Osborne had taken her spirit to Boston where they told her to "hurt the children." After returning to Salem, riding their "stickes or poale," with Good and Osborne behind her holding on to one another, Tituba was taken to the Putnams' household where they made her "hurt the Child," Ann, holding a knife to her throat, and then back to her own house to torment Abigail Williams and Betty Parris. All this time Tituba reported that she had tried to resist and had struggled against the overwhelming strength of the five evil ones. They in turn were assisted by a variety of strange creatures including the wolf that had scared Elizabeth Hubbard.

Suddenly, Elizabeth Hubbard, who was sitting in the Meeting House listening to the questioning, panicked at Tituba's graphic description of these evil beings and a verification of her complaint about a wolf. She fell into "an extreame fit." Pandemonium broke loose as the other girls began to cry out. Tituba was so overcome by this reaction to her story that she appeared to be "once or twice taken dumb herself," [as recorded in *The Salem Witch Papers*]. As Tituba drew into a trance-like silence, the hysteria of the girls heightened. The questioning could not continue. The first examination ended abruptly. . . .

A Pact with the Devil

The next day, March 2, in her second official examination, calm temporarily prevailed and Tituba was finally asked about a covenant with the man. The story became even more elaborate, with Tituba seemingly taking more deliberate steps to frighten her listeners. She said the man had told her he was God. He wanted her to serve him for six years and to hurt the children. In return for signing the pact with him, she would be protected from harm and would receive "many fine things." Asked why she had not informed Parris of these happenings and requested his assistance, Tituba explained that she was sworn to secrecy by the two Salem women, who threatened her life if she revealed their diabolical powers. She was afraid the man "would Cutt [her] head off" if she told. Fear for one's physical safety was an emotion that Puritans could sympathize with.

The officials were shocked and possibly secretly gratified by Tituba's acknowledgment of a covenant with the Devil. They took it as confirmation of their worst fears. Puritan divines had always required evidence not of maleficium—evil action—but of a Satanic influence to convict people of witchcraft. Thus their questioning of suspected witches usually concentrated on their involvement with this diabolical presence and of a conspiracy resulting from it. As a result, the courts were usually unable to secure convictions of accused witches who knew nothing of such a pact. Tituba ostensibly gave them the needed evidence. . . .

Tituba probably knew little about the sophisticated concept of a Devil's pact, which existed only in the minds of her more educated interrogators. Nor did she necessarily conceptualize a Devil's sabbat, that "nightmare of learned witch lore," [as Norman Cohn phrases it]. But she would have been well versed in the institution of servitude and the various levels of bondage in colonial society. Her answers to the question of what kind of "covenant" she had made with "that man that came to you?" was to voice her discontent with her present status and talk about her whimsical hopes for the future embodied in a piece of paper that she could sign. Tituba's response to their questioning was easily the reaction of a slave to the suggestion of a written agreement that could improve her life on earth. . . .

A Conspiracy of Evil

It took a few more leading questions before Tituba, responding to the magistrates' additional promptings regarding a Devil's book, gave her inquisitors more reason to wonder about what was happening in their community. The contract on a piece of paper became a book with many marks. Now, mindful of the power she had to create anxiety and probably with malice in mind, Tituba had added a few more people to the supposed Satanic pact. When asked how many names she saw in the book, she said there were nine marks in the book. It was sufficient evidence to arouse her questioners to the enormity of the conspiracy and further fuel their fears of a pervasive diabolical presence. . . .

Puritan Fantasies Fueled

During the five days of testimony, Tituba and the two other women were taken to jail in Ipswich, about ten miles away from the Salem village meeting house. Daily the constables, on horseback, brought the women back to the village for additional questioning. At some time during that five-day period, they were subjected to at least one minute and humiliating search of their naked bodies, including the genital area, for signs of a "witches' teat" or some mark from which, according to legend, the Devil or his familiars suckled their converts. Such marks had been used traditionally both in England and in New England as empirical evidence of a diabolical association. The examining women thought they saw some telltale sign on Tituba, but it could just as well have been the wounds from a beating shortly before the hearings. It was not there on reexamination.

Tituba's extraordinary message to her examiners was to look among the elite for the evil beings.

The two Sarahs continued to maintain their innocence. But with each session Tituba confirmed with more certainty the evil presence, as she faithfully repeated her early testimony. The Reverend Hale was convinced of her honesty because he assumed she could not have remembered all those extraordinary details if she had been lying. Finally satisfied that she could offer no more information, on March 7 the magistrates sent Tituba and the other two to Boston to await trial and punishment. Sarah Osborne would die in prison on May 10, 1692; Sarah Good would be tried, found guilty, and hanged on July 19. Tituba outlived them, her confession serving as a shield against any immediate drastic action. . . .

By the beginning of June Tituba's testimony apparently was no longer necessary; the details had entered into the folklore of New England witchcraft. Other witnesses, reformulating and embellishing her fantasy of a Satanic pact, would provide sufficient evidence to condemn the innocent to death.

If Tituba had had revenge in mind for her own enslavement, she could not have found a more effective weapon against the community than her fantastic story of a witches' meeting in Boston to plot harmful acts, a compact with an evil being, and a suspicious book with nine names. The magistrates interpreted the details of that confession as proof that the diabolical presence had invaded their community. Tituba had fueled their fantasies of a Satanic plot. As she awaited news of her fate in a Boston jail, the next stage in this witch-hunt, to find those unnamed conspirators and reveal the extent of Satan's influence, was about to begin.

Chapter

What Motivated the "Afflicted" Girls?

1

The Girls Were
Consummate Actresses

Charles W. Upham

Charles W. Upham's 1867 account of the witch scare, *Salem Witchcraft*, was the standard interpretation of the event well into the twentieth century. In this selection from volume two of the study, Upham suggests that the "afflicted" girls were actresses. They enjoyed the attention which their initial antics brought them, but became aware of their very real power only when the first three arrests were made based on their accusations. Having committed themselves to the highly visible and gratifying role of afflicted girls, however, they were reluctant to then admit that they had made up the charges. Upham contends that the girls may have become mentally unstable during the course of the hearings, but that this did not diminish their abilities as actresses.

Charles W. Upham served as a Unitarian minister in Salem, a member of the Massachusetts legislature, and a U.S. congressman. He may also have been the model for the cursed Judge Pyncheon, a character in Nathaniel Hawthorne's 1851 novel of greed, guilt, witchcraft, and reconciliation, *The House of the Seven Gables*.

During the winter of 1691 and 1692, a circle of young girls had been formed, who were in the habit of meeting at Mr. Parris's house for the purpose of practising palmistry, and other arts of fortune-telling, and of becoming experts in the wonders of necromancy, magic, and spiritualism. It consisted, besides the Indian servants [Tituba and John Indian], mainly of the following persons:—

Excerpted from *Salem Witchcraft*, by Charles W. Upham (Boston, MA: Wiggin and Lunt, 1867).

Elizabeth, daughter of Mr. Parris, was nine years of age. She seems to have performed a leading part in the first stages of the affair, and must have been a child of remarkable precocity. It is a noticeable fact, that her father early removed her from the scene. She was sent to the town, where she remained in the family of Stephen Sewall, until the proceedings at the village were brought to a close. Abigail Williams, a niece of Mr. Parris, and a member of his household, was eleven years of age. She acted conspicuously in the witchcraft prosecutions from beginning to end. Ann Putnam, daughter of Sergeant Thomas Putnam, the parish clerk or recorder, was twelve years of age. The character and social position of her parents gave her a prominence which an extraordinary development of the imaginative faculty, and of mental powers generally, enabled her to hold throughout. This young girl is perhaps entitled to be regarded as, in many respects, the leading agent in all the mischief that followed. Mary Walcott was seventeen years of age. Her father was Jonathan Walcott. His first wife, Mary Sibley, to whom he was married in 1664, had died in 1683. She was the mother of Mary. It is a singular fact, and indicates the estimation in which Captain Walcott was held, that, although not a churchmember, he filled the office of deacon of the parish for several years before the formation of the church. Mercy Lewis was also seventeen years of age. When quite young, she was, for a time, in the family of the Rev. George Burroughs: and, in 1692, was living as a servant in the family of Thomas Putnam; although, occasionally, she seems to have lived, in the same capacity, with that of John Putnam, Jr., the constable of the village. He was a son of Nathaniel, and resided in the neighborhood of Thomas and Deacon Edward Putnam. Mercy Lewis performed a leading part in the proceedings, had great energy of purpose and capacity of management, and became responsible for much of the crime and horror connected with them. Elizabeth Hubbard, seventeen years of age, who also occupies a bad eminence in the scene, was a niece of Mrs. Dr. Griggs, and lived in her family. Elizabeth Booth and Susannah Sheldon, each eighteen years of age, belonged to families in the neighborhood. Mary Warren, twenty years of age, was a servant in the family of John Procter; and Sarah Churchill, of the same age, was a servant in that of George Jacobs, Sr. . . .

The Girls Gain Attention

In the course of the winter, they became quite skilful and expert in the arts they were learning, and gradually began to display their attainments to the admiration and amazement of beholders. At first, they made no charges against any person, but confined themselves to strange actions, exclamations, and contortions. They would creep into holes, and under benches and chairs, put themselves into odd and unnatural postures, make wild and antic gestures, and utter incoherent and unintelligible sounds. They would be seized with spasms, drop insensible to the floor, or writhe in agony, suffering dreadful tortures, and uttering loud and piercing outcries. The attention of the families in which they held their meetings was called to their extraordinary condition and proceedings; and the whole neighborhood and surrounding country soon were filled with the story of the strange and unaccountable sufferings of the "afflicted girls." No explanation could be given, and their condition became worse and worse. The physician of the village, Dr. Griggs, was called in, a consultation had, and the opinion finally and gravely given, that the afflicted children were bewitched. . . .

The evidence rather favors the supposition, that the girls originally had no design of accusing, or bringing injury upon, any one. But the ministers at Parris's house, physicians and others, began the work of destruction by pronouncing the opinion that they were bewitched. This carried with it, according to the received doctrine, a conviction that there were witches about; for the Devil could not act except through the instrumentality of beings in confederacy with him. Immediately, the girls were beset by everybody to say who it was that bewitched them. Yielding to this pressure, they first cried out upon such persons as might have been most naturally suggested to them,—Sarah Good, apparently without a regular home, and wandering with her children from house to house for shelter and relief; Sarah Osborne, a melancholy, broken-minded, bed-ridden person; and Tituba, a slave, probably of mixed African and Indian blood.

Power Traps the Girls

At the examination of these persons, the girls were first brought before the public, and the awful power in their hands revealed to them. The success with which they acted their parts; the novelty of the scene; the ceremonials of the occasion, the magistrates in their imposing dignity and authority, the trappings of the marshal and his officers, the forms of proceeding,—all which they had never seen before; the notice taken of them; the importance attached to them; invested the affair with a strange fascination in their eyes, and awakened a new class of sentiments and ideas in their minds. A love of distinction and notoriety, and the several passions that are gratified by the expression by others of sympathy, wonder, and admiration, were brought into play. The fact that all eyes were upon them, with the special notice of the magistrates, and the entire confidence with which their statements were received, flattered and beguiled them. A fearful responsibility had been assumed, and they were irretrievably committed to their position. While they adhered to that position, their power was irresistible, and they were sure of the public sympathy and of being cherished by the public favor. If they faltered, they would be the objects of universal execration and of the severest penalties of law for the wrongs already done and the falsehoods already sworn to. There was no retracing their steps; and their only safety was in continuing the excitement they had raised. New victims were constantly required to prolong the delusion, fresh fuel to keep up the conflagration; and they went on to cry out upon others. With the exception of two of their number [Mary Warren and Sarah Churchill], who appear to have indulged spite against the families in which they were servants, there is no evidence that they were actuated by private grievances or by animosities personal to themselves. They were ready and sure to wreak vengeance upon any who expressed doubts about the truth of their testimony, or the propriety of the proceedings; but, beyond this, they were very indifferent as to whom they should accuse. They were willing, as to that matter, to follow the suggestions of others, and availed themselves of all the gossip and slander and unfriendly talk in their families that reached their ears. It was found, that a hint, with a little information as to persons, places, and circumstances, conveyed to them by those who had resentments and grudges to gratify, would be sufficient for the purpose. . . .

Mental Instability?

In the mean while, they were becoming every day more perfect in the performance of their parts; and their imaginative powers, nervous excitability, and flexibility and rapidity of muscular action, were kept under constant stimulus, and attaining a higher development. The effect of these things, so long continued in connection with the perpetual pretence, becoming more or less imbued with the character of belief, of their alliance and communion with spiritual beings and manifestations, may have unsettled, to some extent, their minds. Added to this, a sense of the horrid consequences of their actions, accumulating with every pang they inflicted, the innocent blood they were shedding, and the depths of ruin into which they were sinking themselves and others, not only demoralized, but to some extent, perhaps, crazed them. . . .

The evidence rather favors the supposition, that the girls originally had no design of accusing, or bringing injury upon, any one.

They followed their victims to the gallows, and jeered, scoffed, insulted them in their dying hours. Sarah Churchill, according to the testimony of Sarah Ingersoll, on one occasion came to herself, and manifested the symptoms of a restored moral consciousness: but it was a temporary gleam, a lucid interval; and she passed back into darkness, continuing, as before, to revel in falsehood, and scatter destruction around her. With this single exception, there is not the slightest appearance of compunction or reflection among them. On the contrary, they seem to have been in a frivolous, sportive, gay frame of thought and spirits. There is, perhaps, in this view of their conduct and demeanor, something to justify the belief that they were really demented. The fact that a large amount of skilful art and adroit cunning was displayed by them is not inconsistent with the supposition that they had become partially insane; for such cunning and art are often associated with insanity. . . .

Superb Actresses

Whatever opinion may be formed of the moral or mental condition of the "afflicted children," as to their sanity and responsibility, there can be no doubt that they were great actors. In mere jugglery and sleight of hand, they bear no mean comparison with the workers of wonders, in that line, of our own day. Long practice had given them complete control over their countenances, intonations of voice, and the entire muscular and nervous organization of their bodies; so that they could at will, and on the instant, go into fits and convulsions, swoon and fall to the floor, put their frames into strange contortions, bring the blood to the face, and send it back again. They could be deadly pale at one moment, at the next flushed; their hands would be clenched and held together as with a vice; their limbs stiff and rigid or wholly relaxed; their teeth would be set; they would go through the paroxysms of choking and strangulation, and gasp for breath, bringing froth and blood from the mouth; they would utter all sorts of screams in unearthly tones; their eyes remain fixed, sometimes bereft of all light and expression, cold and stony, and sometimes kindled into flames of passion; they would pass into the state of somnambulism, without aim or conscious direction in their movements, looking at some point, where there was no apparent object of vision, with a wild, unmeaning glare. There are some indications that they had acquired the art of ventriloquism; or they so wrought upon the imaginations of the beholders, that the sounds of the motions and voices of invisible beings were believed to be heard. They would start, tremble, and be pallid before apparitions, seen, of course, only by themselves; but their acting was so perfect that all present thought they saw them too. They would address and hold colloquy with spectres and ghosts; and the responses of the unseen beings would be audible to the fancy of the bewildered crowd. They would follow with their eyes the airy visions, so that others imagined they also beheld them. This was surely a high dramatic achievement. Their representations of pain, and every form and all the signs and marks of bodily suffering,—as in the case of Ann Putnam's arm, and the indentations of teeth on the flesh in many instances,—utterly deceived everybody. . . .

Our [Puritan] fathers abhorred, with a perfect hatred, all theatrical exhibitions. It would have filled them with horror to propose going to a play. But unwittingly, week after week, month in and month out, ministers, deacons, brethren, and sisters of the church rushed to Nathaniel Ingersoll's [inn], to the village and town meeting-houses, and to Thomas Beadle's Globe Tavern, and gazed with wonder, awe, and admiration upon acting such as has seldom been surpassed on the boards of any theatre, high or low, ancient or modern.

2

Hysteria and Fear of Witchcraft Afflicted the Girls

Chadwick Hansen

Historian Chadwick Hansen contends that the afflicted girls were suffering from clinical hysteria caused by their fear that they were the victims of witchcraft. In this selection from his 1969 book, *Witchcraft at Salem*, Hansen explains that seventeenth-century physicians interpreted many of the symptoms of hysteria as signs that the afflicted individual was a victim of witchcraft. The girls were driven to hysteria, he maintains, in part because belief in witchcraft was widespread at the time, and some people did undoubtedly practice witchcraft. Hansen contends that witchcraft works when people believe it does—in Salem, people's belief in witchcraft resulted in hysteria and psychosomatic fear responses among the afflicted girls.

Early in the year 1692 several girls of Salem Village (now Danvers), Massachusetts, began to sicken and display alarming symptoms. The most disturbing and most frequent of these symptoms was convulsive fits: fits so grotesque and so violent that eyewitnesses agreed the girls could not possibly be acting. "Their motions in their fits," wrote the Reverend Deodat Lawson, "are preternatural, both as to the manner, which is so strange as a well person could not screw their body into; and as to the violence also it is preternatural, being much beyond the ordinary force of the same person when they are in their right mind." The

Reverend John Hale of Beverly confirmed Lawson's description. "Their arms, necks, and backs," he wrote, "were turned this way and that way, and returned back again, so as it was impossible for them to do of themselves, and beyond the power of any epileptic fits, or natural disease to effect."

There were other symptoms almost equally alarming: temporary loss of hearing, speech, and sight; loss of memory, so that some of the girls could not recall what had happened to them in their fits; a choking sensation in the throat; loss of appetite. Later there were terrifying hallucinations; they saw specters who tormented them in a variety of ingenious and cruel ways. They felt themselves pinched and bitten, and often there were actual marks upon the skin.

Clinical Hysteria

These symptoms are readily recognizable. The most cursory examination of the classic studies of hysteria—of [late 19th and early 20th century French and Austrian neurologists Jean and Martin] Charcot, of [Pierre] Janet, of [Josef] Breuer and [Sigmund] Freud—will demonstrate that the afflicted girls of Salem were hysterical in the scientific sense of that term. It has, of course, been customary to call these girls hysterical, but only in the loosest and most popular sense of the word. Thus the same historians who have called them hysterical have also called them liars, although the terms are mutually exclusive so far as conscious motivation is concerned. With minor exceptions the girls' behavior belongs to the history of pathology rather than the history of fraud.

In any case, their behavior was both conspicuous and distressing. Two of them, Elizabeth Parris and Abigail Williams, were the daughter and niece of the Reverend Samuel Parris of Salem Village, and the Reverend Mr. Parris treated their affliction with those universal remedies of seventeenth-century Massachusetts, prayer and fasting. But he also did what you or I would do if our children began behaving in that fashion: he took them to the doctor—to a series of doctors, in fact—and he persuaded other parents and guardians to do the same. For some time the physicians were puzzled, but eventually one of them—tradition says it was Dr. William Griggs of Salem Village—produced a diagnosis. "The evil hand," he announced, "is upon them"; the girls were victims of malefic witchcraft.

Seventeenth-Century Terms for Hysteria

The diagnosis was in no way unusual. The overwhelming majority of seventeenth-century physicians, like other learned men, believed in witchcraft and considered it the cause of some diseases. An instructive parallel to Doctor Griggs's opinion is that of Sir Thomas Browne, the celebrated author of *Religio Medici*, who was called as expert witness by an English witchcraft court convened at Bury St. Edmunds in 1664. He gave as his opinion:

> that these swooning fits were natural, and nothing else but what they call the mother, but only heightened to a great excess by the subtlety of the Devil, co-operating with the malice of these which we term witches, at whose instance he doth these villainies.

"The mother" was the common abbreviation for "the suffocation of the mother," one of the seventeenth-century English terms for hysteria; it referred to the choking sensation in the throat that was one of the commoner symptoms. . . .

Official Views of Witchcraft

Toward the end of the Middle Ages and the beginning of the Renaissance both church and state began to take witchcraft more seriously. The crucial century was the fifteenth, which saw a number of important trials, including those of Joan of Arc, Gilles de Rais, and the Duchess of Gloucester. At the end of this century, in 1490, *Malleus Maleficarum* (*The Hammer of Witches*) was published. The authors were James Sprenger and Henry Kramer, two German Dominicans, and their book was published with the Papal Bull by which Innocent VIII gave them jurisdiction as Inquisitors for the Germanic countries. *Malleus* gave a thorough definition of witchcraft, with rules on how to investigate, try, and judge cases of witchcraft. It remained an important work for more than two hundred years; Increase Mather knew it and referred to it.

The publication of *Malleus Maleficarum* gives us a convenient date for the opening of that general war against the Devil which occupied all Christendom during the sixteenth and seventeenth centuries. The full horror of that warfare will never be known in all of its details. Even the statistics of convicted witches who were executed vary widely from one authority to another. But it is clear that the battle reached its height during the first half of the seventeenth century, when, for example, approximately nine hundred witches were burned in the single city of Bamberg, and approximately five thousand in the single province of Alsace.

Seventeenth-Century Scientists' Views of Witchcraft

It is at first thought surprising that witchcraft executions should have reached their height during the seventeenth century, which was, as we have all been taught, the century that produced most of the seminal ideas of modern science. [Philosopher Alfred North] Whitehead called it "the century of genius," and with good reason. In English science alone it was the time of [Sir Francis] Bacon, who first saw the possibilities of an inductive scientific method; of Robert Boyle, who in *The Skeptical Chemist* replaced the four Aristotelian elements (earth, air, fire, and water) with the modern definition of an element as a chemically irreducible substance, and thus made modern chemistry possible; of [Sir Isaac] Newton, who laid the mathematical and mechanical foundations of classical physics. The difficulty is that we tend to remember these men only for those ideas we still value, forgetting the other contents of their minds.

The afflicted girls of Salem were hysterical in the scientific sense of that term.

We forget that Bacon believed you could cure warts by rubbing them with a rind of bacon and hanging it out of a window that faced south, and that witchcraft may take place "by a tacit operation of malign spirits." We forget that Boyle believed in an astonishing and repulsive variety of medicaments, including stewed earthworms, a worsted stocking that has long been worn next to the flesh, and human urine. The latter substance, taken both internally and externally, was one of the favorite items in his pharmacopoeia; it would, he thought, "require rather a whole book than a part of an essay, to enumerate and insist on" its "medical virtues." It was Boyle who proposed that English miners be interviewed as to whether they "meet with any subterraneous demons; and if they do, in what shape and manner they appear; what they portend, and what they do." And New-ton, the greatest scientist of his age, spent more of his time on the occult than he did in the study of physics. He expli-cated, for example, apocalyptic passages in the Bible, and in-terpreted the measurements of Solomon's temple, hoping in both cases that a mystic reading of the scriptures would lead him to the inmost secrets of the universe.

We should remember also that the seventeenth century firmly believed in a dualistic universe: in a material or visi-ble world, and a spiritual or invisible world as well. Heaven was still a concrete reality, as were the Angels who inhabited it; so was Hell and its Devils. . . .

A Skeptic's Opinion

[Philosopher Thomas] Hobbes was a skeptic, but his skep-ticism was rather different in character from that of the nineteenth or twentieth century. "As for witches," he wrote in his *Leviathan*, "I think not that their witchcraft is any real power; but yet that they are justly punished, for the false be-lief they have that they can do such mischief, joined with their purpose to do it if they can; their trade being nearer to a new religion than to a craft or science."

If you had been sticking pins in your neighbor's image or casting spells on his cow, you would not have wanted Thomas Hobbes to be your judge. He would not have be-lieved in your occult powers, but he would have hanged you anyway, for your heresy and for your malice. What is of im-mediate interest to us, however, is not Hobbes' ferocious-ness, but the degree of his skepticism. He was convinced that witchcraft did not work, but it did not occur to him for one moment to doubt that people practiced it. In fact, no-body in the seventeenth century or before doubted the ex-istence of witchcraft as a common practice; skepticism ex-tended only to the questions of whether it worked, and if so whether by spiritual or natural means, and if those who practiced it should be held legally accountable. . . .

It should be emphasized that all of the learned, whether believers or skeptics in principle, were skeptical of the ma-jority of witchcraft cases that came to their attention, be-cause they were all too well aware of the abysmal depth and infinite extent of popular credulity. Every accident, every sudden or unusual illness of man or of beast, every inex-plicable or menacing circumstance of any sort was apt to raise the cry of witchcraft among the common people. The learned knew this, and were disposed to approach the individual case with skepticism. . . .

How "Witchcraft" Works

We must bear in mind that in a society which believes in witchcraft, it works. If you believe in witchcraft and you discover that someone has been melting your wax image over a slow fire or muttering charms over your nail-parings, the probability is that you will get extremely sick. To be sure, your symptoms will be psychosomatic rather than organic. But the fact that they are obviously not organic will make them only more terrible, since they will seem the result of malefic and demonic power. So it was in seventeenth-century Europe, and so it was in seventeenth-century Massachusetts.

Nobody in the seventeenth century or before doubted the existence of witchcraft as a common practice.

The hideous convulsive fits were thought to be the result of witches and demons wrenching the bodies of their victims into tortuous postures. The loss of hearing, speech, sight, appetite, and memory were deprivations caused by Satan himself. The contraction of the throat—the *globus hystericus*—was seen as an attempt by demons to make the victim swallow occult poisons. And when she swallowed rapidly and her belly swelled (what is actually involved here is a kind of accelerated ulcer formation), it was thought the demons had succeeded. When blisters appeared upon the skin (many skin diseases are functional rather than organic), they were thought to have been raised by brimstone out of Hell. Many of these symptoms, including the skin lesions, would pass fairly rapidly. Cotton Mather, who was a Fellow of the Royal Society, a former medical student, and a thorough and careful observer, remarked more than once on the surprising rapidity with which "witch-wounds" healed. But other symptoms would persist. And a new fit would bring a repetition of the old afflictions, or new ones equally alarming.

The cause of these hysterical symptoms, of course, was not witchcraft itself but the victim's fear of it, and that is why so many innocent persons were executed. It is impossible now, and was in many instances impossible then, to tell how many of the persons executed for witchcraft were actually guilty of practicing it. It is surely no exaggeration to say that the majority, even the vast majority, were innocent victims of hysterical fears. But we should again be wary of converting a statistical truth into a general principle. While it is clearly true that the majority of persons executed for witchcraft were innocent, it is equally true that some of them, in Massachusetts and elsewhere, were guilty.

3

The Putnam Family's Accusations: A Case of Psychological Projection

Paul Boyer and Stephen Nissenbaum

University of Massachusetts professors Paul Boyer and Stephen Nissenbaum collaborated on the seminal study of factional conflict in Salem, *Salem-Village Witchcraft: A Documentary Record of Local Conflict in Colonial New England,* as well as on a study of the social origins of witchcraft, *Salem Possessed.* In this selection from *Salem Possessed,* Boyer and Nissenbaum argue that the women in Thomas Putnam Jr.'s family (his wife Ann Carr Putnam, his daughter Ann, his servant Mercy Lewis, and his niece Mary Walcott) were engaged in a "deadly game of psychological projection." They accused women of being witches who reminded them of the woman most obviously responsible for their economic problems: Mary Veren Putnam. Mary Veren Putnam was Thomas Jr.'s stepmother, and Thomas Jr. believed she had influenced his father into bequeathing the largest part of his estate to herself and to their young son Joseph. Thomas Jr. and his brother Edward were given farms but no fortune in their father's will.

Boyer and Nissenbaum see parallels to the Putnam family crisis in such fairy tales as *Cinderella* and *Hansel and Gretel,* where evil stepmothers and children of first marriages engage in deadly conflict. They maintain that the Putnam women's accusations reveal an increasingly obsessive desire to eliminate psychological equivalents of their own evil stepmother, Mary Veren Putnam.

Excerpted from *Salem Possessed: The Social Origins of Witchcraft,* by Paul Boyer and Stephen Nissenbaum (Cambridge, MA: Harvard University Press, 1974). Copyright © 1974 by the President and Fellows of Harvard College. All rights reserved. Reprinted with permission.

The implications of his father's second marriage for Thomas Putnam, Jr., had deepened immeasurably in 1669 (although the sixteen-year-old youth may not have realized it at the time) with the arrival of Joseph Putnam. Perhaps Mary Veren had acquired some of the business acumen of the Salem circles in which she had moved, or perhaps her new husband had decided on his own to shift his deepest loyalties from the connections of his first marriage to those of his second. In any case, one or both of them began to promote the interests of their son Joseph at the expense of Thomas Putnam's other children, including Thomas, Jr., now on the threshold of manhood. When the elder Thomas Putnam died in 1686, he left a will which bequeathed to Mary *and to Joseph*—then sixteen years old—the best part of his estate, including the ample family homestead, the household furnishings, all the barns and outbuildings, and agricultural equipment (the "plow gear and cart and tackling of all sorts, with all my tools [and] implements of all sorts") and many of the most fertile acres that had been granted to old John Putnam forty years before. . . .

Thomas and Edward were convinced that they had been discriminated against. . . .

Stepmothers and Witches

By 1692 the children of the first Thomas Putnam—and especially his eldest son's family—were prepared to believe that witchcraft lay at the root of their troubles. They were hardly the first, under similar circumstances, to reach such a conclusion. Indeed, this episode in the history of the Putnam family, as well as its tragic denouement, is echoed in what might at first seem the least likely of sources: the folk-literature of medieval Europe, in which the evil stepmother and avaricious half-sibling frequently play central roles. The father of Cinderella, for example, takes as his second wife a widow associated with high society who, with the two daughters of her previous marriage, quickly comes to "govern him entirely" (as Mary Veren was accused of doing with her husband Putnam) and to relegate Cinderella, the child of his first marriage, to the role of a menial.

The parallels are even closer in *Hansel and Gretel*, even though in this most famous witch story of all, the central family (unlike the Putnams) is poor and the stepmother brings no children of her own into the household. But like

Cinderella—and the older children of Thomas Putnam, Sr.—Hansel and Gretel find themselves victimized and exploited by their father's selfish second wife, who ultimately persuades her somewhat reluctant husband to abandon them to certain death in the forest. But a magical bird leads them to a cottage made of bread, cake, and sugar—an impoverished child's image of prosperity. The old witch who lives in the place captures them and treats them precisely as their stepmother had done, exploiting their labor and even plotting their murder. ("Get up, you lazybones," she orders Gretel, "fetch water and cook something for your brother. When he's fat I'll eat him up.") But instead, it is the children who kill the witch, using the method often employed in European witch trials: fire. They return home—no trouble finding their way this time—laden with the "pearls and precious stones" they have discovered hidden in the witch's house. These they show to their overjoyed father, who "had not passed a single happy hour since he left them in the wood" and who informs them that their stepmother has died in their absence. Only the original family is left to share the witch's wealth.

Both structurally and psychologically, the "witch" in *Hansel and Gretel* is a symbolic projection of the stepmother herself. . . .

Strangely enough, the younger Thomas Putnam and his siblings never directly attacked the two persons most obviously responsible for their difficulties: their stepmother and their half-brother. Neither Mary Veren Putnam nor Joseph Putnam was named as a witch in 1692—though family tradition long held that Joseph kept a horse saddled day and night during that summer, and never ventured forth without a gun. But, in the end, his precautions proved unnecessary. Was this because Mary and her son (unlike wealthy persons living outside the Village) were simply too powerful and too immediate a presence to be challenged directly? Or would accusations against them—since they were, in spite of everything, still part of the family—have involved psychic strains too intense to be borne? Whatever the reason, it seems clear that the Putnams in 1692 (like Hansel and Gretel in the folk tale) projected their bitterness onto persons who were, politically or psychologically, less threatening targets: notably older women of Mary Veren Putnam's generation. Against such persons they vented the rage and bitterness which they were forced to deny (or to channel through such stylized outlets as legal petitions) in their relations with Mary and Joseph.

The Accusation of Martha Corey

The original "afflictions," though evidently beginning in the Parris household, quickly spread from there to the three girls who lived in the household of Thomas Putnam, Jr.: Ann, Mary, and Mercy. But the imprisonment of the first three accused witches on March 1, Sarah Good, Sarah Osborne, and Tituba, did not cause the symptoms to abate. Indeed, they now spread to Thomas's wife, Ann Putnam, Sr. By the second week in March, both mother and daughter were complaining that they were being tortured by another woman, Martha Corey. The sufferings of the elder Ann Putnam became especially acute on the afternoon of the eighteenth: already "wearied out in helping to tend my poor afflicted child and maid," Mrs. Putnam was just lying down in bed "to take a little rest" when Goody Corey's apparition appeared and "torture[d] me so as I cannot express, ready to tear me all to pieces."

[Ann Putnam, Mary Putnam, and Mercy Lewis] were driven to lash out at persons of real respectability—persons, in short, who reminded them of the individuals actually responsible (so they believed) for their own reduced fortunes.

Like the three women already in prison, there was a taint about Martha Corey: she had given birth, years earlier, to an illegitimate mulatto son, and the young man was still living in the Corey household, just over the Village line in Salem Town, with Martha and her second husband, Giles Corey. (Martha's first husband had been a Salem Townsman named Rich—like Mary Veren she had come as a mature woman to Salem Village after having been long identified with Salem Town.) But Goody Corey was not simply another Village outcast like Sarah Good or Tituba, for her husband was a prospering though somewhat obstreperous farmer and landowner, and—a fact of considerable importance—Martha herself was a covenanting member of the Salem Village church.

The accusation of such a person as Martha Corey was a key point along the psychological progression which the Thomas Putnam family, and the entire witchcraft episode, followed in 1692. For in turning on her they betrayed the fact that witchcraft accusations against the powerless, the outcast, or the already victimized were not sufficiently cathartic for them. They were driven to lash out at persons of real respectability—persons, in short, who reminded them of the individuals actually responsible (so they believed) for their own reduced fortunes and prospects. Martha Corey was the ideal transition figure: she combined respectability with a touch of deviance. If the Putnams could bring her down, they would be free, not only politically, but psychologically as well, to play out their compulsions on a still larger scale.

And they brought her down in less than two weeks. On March 19, on the strength of Edward Putnam's complaint that she had afflicted Thomas Putnam's wife and daughter, Martha Corey was arrested. Others would subsequently testify against her, but initially—unlike the first three accused women—she was a Putnam family witch pure and simple.

Rebecca Nurse Is Accused

For their next play in this deadly game of psychological projection, the Putnams moved further up the social and economic ladder—and thus, in a sense, that much closer to Mary Veren Putnam. It was as early as March 13 that the younger Ann Putnam first saw the new and strange female apparition. "I did not know what her name was then," she later testified, "though I knew where she used to sit in our meetinghouse." On the fifteenth, Samuel Parris's niece saw the same specter, and four days later, it appeared to Ann Putnam, Sr. By this time its identity had somehow been ascertained: it was Rebecca Nurse, a respected older woman of Salem Village, and the wife of Francis Nurse, a once-obscure artisan who in 1678 had established himself as a substantial figure in the Village by purchasing, on credit, a rich, 300-acre farm near the Ipswich Road.

Rebecca was convicted largely on the basis of spectral afflictions which befell the elder Ann Putnam between March 19 and 24, 1692. At first, until Martha Corey was imprisoned, Rebecca was distinctly a secondary figure in Ann Putnam's roster of spectral visitors. But after the twenty-first, with Corey safely in prison, Goody Nurse became the dominant presence in Ann's life. On Tuesday March 22, as Mrs. Putnam would later testify, her apparition "set upon me in a most dreadful manner, very early in the morning, as soon as it was well light." The struggle which ensued, and which was to continue almost without respite for three days, was at once physical and spiritual. Dressed at first "only in her shift," Nurse carried in her hand the morning of her first visitation to the Putnam household a "little red book" which she "vehemently" urged Mistress Ann to sign (to sign away what? her soul? her estate?). When Ann refused, the specter (as she put it) "threatened to tear my soul out of my body," and denied that God had any power to save her. The ordeal lasted almost two hours, and it recurred intermittently for the rest of the day. . . .

Rebecca Nurse Resembles Mary Veren Putnam

The encounter between Ann Putnam, Sr., and "Rebecca Nurse" is the most vivid and intimate record we have of the actual process by which a "witch" was singled out for accusation, and of the degree to which the accusers felt palpably threatened by the specters which haunted them. In retrospect, perhaps, Rebecca Nurse appears the inevitable victim, since she was an ideal "substitute" for Mary Veren Putnam: both were women of advanced years, both were prosperous and respected, both were in failing health, and both were members of the Salem Town church (though Rebecca occasionally worshiped in the Village).

To be sure, there were also a number of reasons, on the conscious and "rational" level, why Ann Putnam may have resented and even feared Rebecca Nurse. Rebecca was from Topsfield, whose town authorities had for years been harassing the Putnam family by claiming that parts of their lands actually lay in Topsfield rather than in Salem Village. And her husband Francis had been involved during the 1670's in a protracted dispute with Nathaniel Putnam over some mutually bounded acreage. Furthermore, Francis Nurse, though not a real leader in Village politics, was clearly identified with the faction which the Putnams opposed. Along with Joseph Putnam, Daniel Andrew, and Joseph Porter, he had been elected to the anti-Parris Village Committee which took power at the end of 1691. And it was around the Rebecca Nurse case that Israel Porter was soon to try to rally opposition to the trials. Finally, even more than Martha Corey, and through no doing of her own, Rebecca was particularly vulnerable in 1692: years earlier, her mother had been accused of witchcraft (though never arrested or brought to trial) and local gossip had it that the taint had been passed on to her daughters. (Indeed, probably because the accusations against Rebecca jogged memories about the earlier episode, her two sisters were later accused as well.)

Ann Putnam was unable or unwilling publicly to vent her terrible rage on its living source: her mother-in-law Mary Veren Putnam.

But while such circumstances made Rebecca Nurse an acceptable and even plausible "witch" once she had been accused, they did not themselves provide the emotional impetus which led to her being singled out in the first place. The source of that drive lay in the fact that Ann Putnam was unable or unwilling publicly to vent her terrible rage on its living source: her mother-in-law Mary Veren Putnam. . . . Of this redirected rage, Rebecca Nurse, like Martha Corey before her, was the innocent victim.

Ann's Obsession Reveals Rage and Guilt

Once Rebecca *had* been singled out, and Ann Putnam's spectral struggle with her had begun, Ann's frantic monologues reveal a great deal about the nature of her obsession: "I know what you would have . . . , but it is out of your reach," she insists. "[W]e judged she meant her soul," interpolated [Reverend] Deodat Lawson (a little defensively?) at this point in his published report of the interview; but Ann's own words remain laden with unconscious ambiguity. Indeed, it is surprising how little energy Ann devoted during these hours of her travail to accusing Rebecca of witchcraft: it is "Rebecca's" death (or, more specifically, the obliteration of her psychological presence) which obsessed her. "Be gone! Be gone! Be gone!" she cries; "Be gone, do not torment me." She insists that Rebecca's name has been "blotted out" of God's mind forever. She even ventures a prediction: her spectral visitor has "about two years to live." (In fact the guess was only a little optimistic: Mary Veren Putnam survived for almost exactly three years.)

But there is guilt as well as rage in all of this: for when the family of Thomas Putnam was deprived of its birthright . . . it was forced openly and perhaps even consciously to confront the fact that it cared, and cared profoundly, about money and status. The apparition which for six days urged Ann Putnam to "yield to her hellish temptations," and which denied, as Ann put it, "the power of the Lord Jesus to save my soul," was, after all, in the mind of Mrs. Putnam herself. Did she fear that, covenanting church member or no, she had indeed lost her soul?—that it was she and her husband, with their open and drawn-out pursuit of money through the county courts, who were the real witches?

Might any of the other Putnams—or Lawson himself—have sensed danger here? In any case, by this time, the family had seen (and heard) enough. Later that same day, March 23, Edward and Jonathan Putnam went to the officials to swear out a complaint against Goody Nurse, and a warrant for her arrest was issued on the spot. Rebecca's public examination was held the next day. But although the scene had shifted from Ann Putnam's bedroom to the Village meetinghouse, Ann still dominated it. She called out to Rebecca (in what must have been their first non-spectral encounter in some time): "Did you not bring the Black Man with you? Did you not bid me tempt God and die? How often have you eat and drunk your own damnation?"

At this, the exhausted Mrs. Putnam fell into still another fit; with the permission of the presiding magistrates her husband Thomas carried her home. Almost as soon as Rebecca was imprisoned, the elder Ann Putnam's afflictions ceased—and they would not return for over two months. For a while, at least, the obsessive presence of Mary Veren, and all she represented in the life of Thomas Putnam, Jr., and his family, had been exorcised. . . .

Most Salem Village farmers must have found the forces which threatened them amorphous and difficult to pin down; for the Putnams, however, that task was all too easy: it was Mary Veren and her son Joseph who were the serpents in Eden, and if they, or their psychological equivalents, could only be eliminated, all might again be well.

The Girls' Possession Was a Response to Stifling Social Conditions

Carol F. Karlsen

Carol F. Karlsen, a professor of history at the University of Michigan, considers the afflictions suffered by the girls in Salem signs of social discontent. In this selection from her 1987 book, *The Devil in the Shape of a Woman*, Karlsen describes possession as a cultural phenomenon by which women subconsciously rebel against their subordinate position in patriarchal societies. She maintains that the women who became possessed felt discontented with their "place in the divinely planned social order." According to Karlsen, the best example of this discontent was Elizabeth Knapp, who enacted her struggle in 1672. She concludes that the physical behaviors of possession reveal the emotional anguish some women experience when they are torn between the need to accept a male-centered religious and social order and the desire to rebel against these hierarchies.

P ossession, whether in colonial New England or in other societies in which it still occurs, is a collective as well as an individual phenomenon. It affects women primarily, and frequently spreads among groups of women, as it did in Connecticut in 1662–63 and Massachusetts in 1692–93. Individual females undergo the experience, and events in their personal histories help explain it, but the larger meaning of possession is cultural. There are patterns in the behavior of the possessed: the words and actions are learned, and they vary in only minor ways from one individual to another. To explain New England possession, then, we must consider it first as a cultural performance, a symbolic religious ritual through which a series of shared meanings were communicated—by the possessed women themselves, by the ministers who interpreted their words and behavior, and by the community audience for the dramatic events.

Signs of Possession

The first signs of possession, the ministers tell us, were sometimes ambiguous, as when sixteen-year-old Elizabeth Knapp of Groton, who became possessed in 1672, began [in the words of Reverend Samuel Willard] "to carry herself in a strange and unwonted manner," giving occasional shrieks and then breaking into peals of laughter. More often, compelling physical evidence was present from the start. This typically included strange fits, with violent, contorted body movements; prolonged trances and paralyzed limbs; difficulty in eating, breathing, seeing, hearing, and speaking; sensations of being beaten, pricked with pins, strangled, or stabbed; grotesque screams and pitiful weeping, punctuated by a strange but equally unsettling calm between convulsions, when little if anything was remembered and nothing seemed amiss. . . .

Elizabeth Knapp's possession was the result of her ambivalence about the kind of woman she wanted to be.

Whatever else these young women were experiencing (and that is a separate issue), they and the people around them understood their behavior in terms of their religious beliefs. Witches, acting as Satan's agents, were tempting young females to join Satan's forces. When these females resisted, they were physically attacked, and possession was the visible sign of both that resistance and that attack. When a witch (or the Devil) stuck pins into the body of one of the possessed, she was [according to Reverend Cotton Mather] "miserably hurt with Pins which were found stuck into her Neck, Back and Arms." When a witch (or the Devil) pinched one of the possessed, "black and blew marks of the pinches became immediately visible unto the standers by." When a witch (or the Devil) would "Flash upon [a possessed person] the Flames of a Fire," observers "saw not the Flames" but the "Blisters thereby Raised upon her" and smelled the brimstone. Neither the ministers who confirmed these tortures nor the other witnesses actually saw witches or the Devil, but they did see the afflictions that resulted and that left them little if any doubt as to their cause. Equally convinced were the possessed themselves, who not only saw their tormentors but felt the excruciating pain. . . .

Possession as a Symptom of Discontent

Were it simply a theological issue for the females involved, they never would have become possessed: they accepted the tenets of their faith as much as anyone around them. But the issues were more complicated for them, and their conflicts more immediate and more personal. Witness Elizabeth Knapp's struggle in 1672, described in detail by her pastor, Groton's Samuel Willard.

Elizabeth Knapp was forced to work out her conflicts with the Devil himself. According to Willard, in one of her early fits, "in which she was violent in bodily motions . . . in roarings and screamings, representing a dark resemblance of hellish torments," she frequently cried out "'money, money,' sometimes 'sin and misery'" along with other, unrecorded words. She tried to blame her condition on an older woman in town, but because Willard did not think the woman a witch, he did not heed Knapp's accusation. Under pressure to reveal the "true and real occasion" of her fits, she declared that the Devil had appeared to her many times over the previous three years, that he offered to make her a witch, and that he proffered to her "money, silks, fine clothes, ease from labor, to show her the whole world, etc." She admitted that the Devil came because of her discontent, and that he came more frequently once she started to work as a servant in the Willard household—a household much more prosperous than her own. She further confessed that she was tempted to murder her own parents, her neighbors, the Willard children, "especially the youngest," and herself. She vehemently denied, at least at first, having signed a covenant with Satan. . . .

In his final remarks, Willard cast Knapp's behavior in terms of the Puritan view of possession. Although reluctant to pass authoritative judgement on what he had witnessed for the preceding two and a half months, he clearly believed that Knapp's "distemper" was both real and diabolical and that the Devil was actually present within her. . . .

Knapp was not simply an innocent victim. Her dissatisfaction had brought the Devil to her, and that moral ultimately had to be communicated. "She is a monument of divine severity," Willard concluded, "and the Lord grant that all that see or hear may fear and tremble."

Discontent as a Sin

From the Puritan perspective, Elizabeth Knapp's possession was the result of her ambivalence about the kind of woman she wanted to be. Had she been willing to rest satisfied with her lack of financial resources, with her work as a servant, and with her limited horizons, she would not have become possessed. The sin that brought the Devil to her was discontent with her condition, with her place in the divinely planned social order. It was the same sin that defined other, older women as witches and therefore, not surprisingly, the one that led Knapp at times to see herself as a witch. But for Puritans, possession was not itself witchcraft, only the potential for witchcraft. Ministers could prevent the onset of witchcraft by helping the possessed adjust to their place in society. In Knapp's case the Devil was able to take advantage of her discontent by attracting her with the things she most desired and leading her to commit (or to the brink of committing) other sins identified with witches, but he was not able to win her completely. Despite Willard's fears, Knapp never became a witch; she married and lived out her life as befitted a good Puritan wife and mother. So successfully did she obliterate her discontent and internalize her culture's model of virtuous womanhood that she almost completely disappears from the public records after 1673.

None of the other descriptions of New England possession are as revealing as Willard's account of the Elizabeth Knapp's struggle, but they do disclose the parallels between Knapp's experience and the possession of other young women. For instance, other possessed females and their ministers obviously shared with Knapp and Willard the belief that witches and the Devil focused their appeals on women's discontents and that in their fits the possessed were tempted to become witches. Yet Knapp was exceptional in acknowledging her discontents openly. Only occasionally did possessed females reveal the specific temptations laid before them. Most often, they portrayed themselves simply as hapless victims, referring vaguely to how they were tempted with "fine things," "comforts," or "the world." Nineteen-year-old Mercy Lewis could only report that her former master George Burroughs "caried me up to an exceeding high mountain and shewed me all the kingdoms of the earth and tould me that he would give them all to me if I would writ in his book. . . ." Mercy Short provided as detailed a description as Knapp's about what was offered to her if she would become a witch—a husband and fine clothes, among other things—but she never explained why she was singled out to be offered these things.

Possession. . . was a dramatic religious ritual through which young females publicly enacted their struggle to avoid internalizing the evil of witchcraft.

In other ways, however, either the possessed themselves or other colonists alluded to female dissatisfactions. Although describing it as a "vain curiosity," minister John Hale noted that in 1692 several young possessed females in Salem were unhappy with their marriage prospects and just before their first fits had resorted to divination to find out their future husbands' occupations. Similarly, Ann Cole of Hartford revealed that her mind was on her marital status when she became possessed in 1662; she was concerned, she said, not only that witches were afflicting her body but that they were trying "to spoile her name, hinder her marriage, etc." Martha Godwin and her younger brothers and sister were unhappy with the tasks required of them in their household; during their possessions, Cotton Mather observed, "whatever Work they were bid to do," the specific limbs necessary to do it became so paralyzed that it was impossible for them to proceed. Nearly all of the possessed registered their discontent with their religious training. Once possessed, they shared Elizabeth Knapp's deep aversion to the word of God—and to the ministers who revealed the word to them.

The reluctance of the possessed to admit their discontent is not surprising in light of the disapprobation female dissatisfaction drew in Puritan culture. To acknowledge those feelings could, as it did with Elizabeth Knapp, convert the fear into the certainty that one was a witch. Possession rituals were supposed to do just the opposite: to convince young women that the danger lay outside them, not within. The line between the two conceptions was a thin one, however, and many people, both possessed and not, could not always draw this distinction. Once the danger was identified as discontent *within* the possessed, they became vulnerable to witchcraft accusations, either from others or from themselves. . . .

Possession, then, was a dramatic religious ritual through which young females publicly enacted their struggle to avoid internalizing the evil of witchcraft. The many reenactments of this performance not only lent Puritan doctrine a symbolic sanction, it also affirmed the social hierarchy of colonial New England. By employing the language of possession in their sermons and writings—complete with witches and demons—ministers doubtless hoped to save their young charges from damnation. At the same time, they ensured that the desire of some females to escape their subordination was never clearly articulated, and their many dissatisfactions never specifically addressed. . . .

Unconscious Rebellion

Possession appears to be a special, altered state of consciousness which some women enter as an involuntary reaction to profound emotional conflict. This conflict emerges from the need simultaneously to embrace social norms and to rebel against them—to live out more autonomous, self-directed lives. With no legitimate way to express this conflict directly, the unbearable psychic tensions are expressed physically—through women's bodies.

The New England possessed were frequently unable to speak: their tongues curled upward toward the roofs of their mouths or curled downward and outward to extraordinary lengths; their throats were constricted or swelled to many times their normal sizes; their words would not come, however hard they tried to speak, and their breath simply would not catch. They strove to communicate through these many physical disabilities what they so much wanted but so much feared to say: that their situations enraged them. Their fits expressed that rage, but not in a way that brought to the surface of normal consciousness the enormous psychic pain that they were experiencing. Their "socially constructed selves" had not been—and could not be—totally obliterated.

The same kind of symbolic expression is apparent in the other physical manifestations of possession. Their hearing impaired, or lost in a trance, the possessed simply could not hear the accustomed call to duty. Their arms, legs, or hands paralyzed, they simply could not do the spinning, sweeping, hauling, and serving customarily required of them. When pinched, bitten, and beaten by forces others could not see or touch, they expressed both their sense of victimization and their own desire to attack the sometimes barely visible and equally untouchable sources of their frustrations. In their complaints of being starved, and in their inability to eat for days on end, they spoke to the depths of their emotional hunger and deprivation, perhaps as well to the denial of their sexual appetites. Both the emotional and the sexual seem to be represented in their overpowering convulsions, the symbolic release of their many pent-up tensions.

Possession appears to be a special, altered state of consciousness which some women enter as an involuntary reaction to profound emotional conflict.

This physical response to their plight would have been most common in women raised in particularly religious households. They were the ones who were most pressured to internalize their society's values, who most frequently heard their parents and ministers warning them of the dangers of rebelling against God's laws. And they had the most to lose by overt rebellion. If these women allowed their conflicts to surface in any other manner, they risked not only society's vengeance but also the loss of approval and love of the people closest to them—most particularly their own fathers or the godly men whom many of the possessed identified as fathers. Elizabeth Knapp was probably not alone in her fear that her extraordinary anger would alienate the man who seemed both to care the most and to insist most strongly on her self-renunciation.

Witchcraft, Possession, and Female Dissatisfaction

Witchcraft possession in early New England, then, was an interpretation placed upon a physical and emotional response to a set of social conditions that had no intrinsic relationship to witches or the Devil. These conditions were in some respect specific to Puritan New England, but they are also evident in other societies. Like women in other times and places, the New England possessed were rebelling against pressures to internalize stifling gender and class hierarchies. Puritans understood that reaction as "witchcraft possession" or "diabolical possession"; other historical and contemporary cultures call it "spirit possession." In modern Western cultures, it is called "hysteria" or some other form of individual psychopathology. The specific label, however, only tells us how certain cultures resist the knowledge of female dissatisfaction and anger with their condition.

Like women in other societies, the New England possessed were able, through this culturally sanctioned physical and emotional response, to affect some of these hierarchical arrangements, if only temporarily. They were also able to focus the community's concern on their difficulties. For once, they were the main actors in the social drama. And the more attention they received, the more they dramatized their socially generated anguish and their internally generated desire to rebel. As the community looked on, their bodies expressed what they otherwise could not: that the enormous pressures put upon them to accept a religiously based, male-centered social order was more than they could bear. To accept the community's truth was to deny the self. To assert the self was to suffer the response of a threatened community. Given this choice, they chose a world of their own.

This world, though, offered no real escape. Their religious beliefs led the possessed finally to confirm the only reality their culture allowed, the reality articulated by their ministers and affirmed by most men and women in their communities. There were only two kinds of women: godly women and witches. If witches symbolized female resistance to this dualism, so too did the possessed. But the possessed also represented female capitulation.

5

The Girls Were Bewitched

Cotton Mather

Although Boston minister Cotton Mather may not have been the fanatic instigator of the Salem witch-hunt that his detractors suggest, he had studied witchcraft and possession cases for years. Mather considered the outbreak of witchcraft in 1692 a plague of evil sent by the Devil to persecute godly Puritans.

In response to Governor Phips's request for an account of the witchcraft trials, Mather asked the clerk of the court, Stephen Sewall, to share his notes and observations about the trials. From Sewall's notes and his own thoughts and observations, Mather composed "The Wonders of the Invisible World" in October 1692. The following excerpts from "Wonders" reveal Mather's clear sense that the afflicted girls were bewitched and that women such as Martha Carrier were justly convicted for witchcraft.

I. Martha Carrier was Indicted for the Bewitching of certain Persons, according to the Form usual in such Cases. Pleading Not Guilty, to her Indictment, there were First brought in a considerable number of the Bewitched Persons; who not only made the Court sensible of an horrid Witchcraft committed upon them, but also deposed, That it was Martha Carrier, or her Shape, that Grievously Tormented them, by Biting, Pricking, Pinching, and Choaking of them. It was further deposed, that while this Carrier was on her Examination, before the Magistrates, the

Excerpted from "The Wonders of the Invisible World," by Cotton Mather, *Narrative of the Witchcraft Cases, 1648–1706*, edited by George Lincoln Burr (New York: Charles Scribner's Sons, 1914).

Poor People were so Tortured that every one expected their Death upon the very Spott; but that upon the binding of Carrier they were eased. Moreover the Look of Carrier then laid the Afflicted People for Dead; and her Touch, if her Eye at the same Time were off them, raised them again. Which things were also now seen upon her Trial. And it was Testifyed, that upon the mention of some having their Necks twisted almost round, by the Shape of this Carrier, she replyed, "Its no matter, tho' their Necks had been twisted quite off."

II. Before the Trial of this prisoner, several of her own Children had frankly and fully confessed, not only that they were Witches themselves, but that this their Mother had made them so. This Confession they made with great shows of Repentance, and with much Demonstration of Truth. They Related Place, Time, Occasion; they gave an account Of Journeyes, Meetings, and Mischiefs by them performed; and were very credible in what they said. Nevertheless, this Evidence was not produced against the Prisoner at the Bar, inasmuch as there was other Evidence enough to proceed upon. . . .

VIII. One Foster, who confessed her own Share in the Witchcraft for which the Prisoner stood indicted, affirm'd, That she had seen the Prisoner at some of their Witch-Meetings, and that it was this Carrier, who perswaded her to be a Witch. She confessed, That the Devil carry'd them on a Pole, to a Witch-Meeting; but the Pole broke, and she hanging about Carriers Neck, they both fell down, and she then Received an Hurt by the Fall, whereof she was not at this very time Recovered.

IX. One Lacy, who likewise confessed her share in this Witchcraft, now Testify'd, That she and the Prisoner were once Bodily present at a Witch-meeting in Salem-Village; and that she knew the Prisoner to be a Witch, and to have been at a Diabolical Sacrament, and that the Prisoner was the undoing of her and her Children, by Enticing them into the Snare of the Devil.

X. Another Lacy, who also Confessed her share in this Witchcraft, now Testify'd, That the Prisoner was at the Witch-Meeting, in Salem Village, where they had Bread and Wine Administred unto them.

XI. In the Time of this Prisoner's Trial, one Susanna Shelden in open Court had her Hands Unaccountably Ty'd together with a Wheel-band, so fast that without Cutting it could not be Loosed: It was done by a Spectre; and the Sufferer affirm'd, it was the Prisoners.

Memorandum. This Rampant Hag, Martha Carrier, was the Person, of whom the Confessions of the Witches, and of her own Children among the rest, agreed, That the Devil had promised her, she should be Queen of Hell.

Other Curiosities About Witches

Having thus far done the Service imposed upon me, I will further pursue it, by relating a few of those Matchless Curiosities, with which the Witchcraft now upon us has entertained us. And I shall Report nothing but with Good Authority, and what I would Invite all my Readers to examine, while tis yet Fresh and New, that if there be found any mistake, it may be as willingly Retracted, as it was unwillingly Committed. . . .

In all the Witchcraft which now Grievously Vexes us, I know not whether any thing be more Unaccountable, than the Trick which the Witches have, to render themselves and their Tools Invisible. . . .

First One of our Bewitched people was cruelly assaulted by a Spectre, that, she said, ran at her with a Spindle: tho' no body else in the Room, could see either the Spectre or the Spindle. At last, in her miseries, giving a Snatch at the

People feared the accused because they were believed to have magical powers used for evil deeds.

Spectre, she pull'd the Spindle away; and it was no sooner got into her hand, but the other people then present beheld, that it was indeed a Real, Proper, Iron Spindle, belonging they knew to whom; which when they Lock'd up very safe, it was nevertheless by Dæmons unaccountably stole away, to do further mischief.

Secondly, Another of our Bewitched People was haunted with a most abusive Spectre, which came to her, she said, with a Sheet about her. After she had undergone a deal of Teaze, from the Annoyances of the Spectre, she gave a Violent Snatch at the Sheet that was upon it; wherefrom she tore a Corner, which in her Hand immediately became Visible to a Roomful of Spectators; a Palpable Corner of a Sheet. Her Father, who was now holding her, Catch'd that he might Keep what his Daughter had so strangely Seized, but the unseen Spectre had like to have pull'd his Hand off, by Endeavouring to wrest it from him; however he still held it, and I suppose has it still to show; it being but a few Hours ago, namely about the Beginning of this October, that this Accident happened; in the family of one Pitman, at Manchester. . . .

Thus the Story.

The Reverend and Worthy Author, having at the Direction of His Excellency the Governour, so far Obliged the Publick, as to give some Account of the Sufferings brought upon the Countrey by Witchcraft; and of the Trials which have passed upon several Executed for the Same:

Upon Perusal thereof, We find the Matters of Fact and Evidence, Truly reported. And a Prospect given, of the Methods of Conviction, used in the Proceedings of the Court at Salem.

Boston Octob 11.   WILLIAM STOUGHTON
        1692.   SAMUEL SEWALL.

Chapter

Why Would the Innocent Confess?

1

The Psychological Pressure to Confess During the Hearings

Paul Boyer and Stephen Nissenbaum

In their introduction to *The Salem Witchcraft Papers*, Amherst professors Paul Boyer and Stephen Nissenbaum explain that the central purpose of the witchcraft trials was to extract confessions. The Court of Oyer and Terminer (to hear and determine), established by Governor William Phips in May 1692, began formal hearings on June 2, 1692. To surmount the problem of spectral evidence, the court needed confessions. Boyer and Nissenbaum contend that intense psychological pressure during these hearings moved many of the accused to confess. For example, defendants who claimed innocence provoked the afflicted girls to experience agonizing convulsions; defendants who confessed guilt released the girls from their agony and sometimes earned the girls' forgiveness.

Ironically, confessions also saved defendants from execution. Presumably held to provide testimony against other accused witches who were reluctant to confess, all of those who confessed were still alive when Governor Phips appointed a special court of judicature in October 1692 which acquitted forty-nine of the confessing witches; Governor Phips reprieved the other three, and three months later he pardoned all others still awaiting trial.

M ay 1692. The prisons were filled, but still not a single witch had been executed—or even brought to trial.

Indeed, there *could* be no trials, for during these months Massachusetts was in the awkward position of being without a legally established government! Eight years earlier, in 1684, the colony's original charter had been abrogated by the English authorities in favor of direct royal control, and in 1689 the governor who had been installed by the English monarch James II was himself overthrown in a bloodless coup—Massachusetts' small-scale version of the Glorious Revolution that cost James his crown and brought William and Mary to the throne in London. Between 1689 and 1691 the colonists had lobbied at court for a restoration of the original charter, but in vain. Under these touchy circumstances it was impossible, especially in a life-and-death matter such as this, to proceed with the prosecution and trials of the accused witches. Ironically, then, one of the most severe challenges ever to confront the Massachusetts judicial system came at a moment when that system was nearly immobilized. For a crucial three-month period, the authorities had no official recourse but to throw suspected witches in jail without a trial.

Although witchcraft was one of the most heinous of all crimes, it was also one of the most difficult to prove, since so much of it took place in the mind of the witch.

Such was the situation that confronted the new governor who had at last been appointed by the royal authorities, Sir William Phips, when he sailed into Boston harbor on May 14, 1692, a new charter safely secured in his sea chest. Phips' response, as he later reported it rather smugly to his superiors in London, was swift and bold, if of dubious legality. Within a few days of his arrival he constituted six members of his advisory council as a special Court of Oyer and Terminer (an ancient but infrequently used English judicial instrument) to "hear and determine" the enormous backlog of witchcraft cases. As chief justice of this court he named his lieutenant governor (and ambitious rival) William Stoughton. The Massachusetts attorney general, Thomas Newton, was dispatched to Salem to prepare the prosecution; a jury was empanelled; and on Friday, June 2, the Court of Oyer and Terminer held its first session in

Salem Town. A single case was carefully selected for this first trial: that of Bridget Bishop, who had been in prison since April 18, and against whom a particularly damning array of evidence had been assembled.

The Problem of Spectral Evidence

Since the deliberations of the Court of Oyer and Terminer have not survived, we do not know how much weight was given to the various kinds of evidence. This was a crucial point, for although witchcraft was one of the most heinous of all crimes, it was also one of the most difficult to prove, since so much of it took place in the mind of the witch. Indeed, the quest for credible evidence helps us understand much in *The Salem Witchcraft Papers* that might otherwise seem puzzling, bizarre, or merely "quaint." As the reader of these documents will at once realize, the form of evidence that constituted the great bulk of the 1692 testimony was that known as *spectral*. This is the testimony that recurs again and again in almost every case, and which the group of "afflicted girls" so unfailingly supplied.

What *was* spectral evidence? As we have already pointed out, the contract between witch and devil was believed to permit the latter to appear in the witch's bodily shape to do the witch's evil bidding. Frequently these shapes, or *specters*, attempted actual bodily harm, as John Cooke's testimony against Bridget Bishop vividly reveals:

> One morning about sun rising, as I was in bed before I rose, I saw Goodwife Bishop [that is, her specter] . . . stand in the chamber by the window. And she looked on me and grinned on me, and presently struck me on the side of the head, which did very much hurt me. And then I saw her go out under the end window at a little crevice about so big as I could thrust my hand into.

In its dense specificity—the precise time, the grin, the blow, the partially opened window—such testimony possessed a superficial resemblance to firm empirical evidence. But, as people came increasingly to recognize in 1692, spectral evidence was seriously flawed in at least two ways. The first problem was a practical one: spectral testimony remained almost impossible to verify, since often only the person experiencing the vision could see it—others in the same room might look and discern nothing. . . .

But spectral evidence posed a still more fundamental problem—a theological one, really: how could one be certain that Satan, in his vast and malevolent power, was not able to assume the shape of an innocent or even a godly person? Had not the Biblical witch of Endor, after all (as accused witch Susannah Martin shrewdly pointed out during her examination in 1692), called up the devil in the shape of the sainted prophet Samuel? Thus, even though the *results* of the spectral crime—the agonies of the children, for example—seemed unquestionably a matter of witchcraft, it was difficult to connect those results absolutely with a specific accused individual. At Bridget Bishop's public examination in Salem Village on April 19, for example, there was no doubt that the afflicted girls were "greatly tormented": when Bishop lifted her eyes, the girls' eyes rolled up into their sockets; when she shook her head, the girls' heads lolled grotesquely from side to side. But what was the proof that Goodwife Bishop was actually *willing* these torments, or that her gestures were being made with malevolent intent? "You seem to act witchcraft before us, by the motion of your body," one magistrate charged—but how could he be certain? . . .

Physical Evidence

Whenever possible, the authorities tried to buttress this testimony with pieces of physical evidence that could, with even greater certitude, be directly linked to the accused witch. For example, one of the most damaging pieces of evidence against Bishop was the puppet with pins stuck in it that a workman and his son had found in the basement of her house some years before. Puppets and pins were an established part of witch lore: the witch supposedly fashioned images of her enemies, stuck pins in them, and thereby spectrally inflicted actual pain on the actual bodies. A puppet was a reassuringly concrete object, and what possible innocent explanation could there be for its presence in Bishop's possession? . . .

Another tell-tale physical sign of guilt, many believed, was the "witch's tit," an unnatural bodily excrescence, often around the genitals, through which the witch or wizard supposedly suckled her or his "familiar"—a demon in the shape of a bird, turtle, or monstrous hybrid that gained its nutriment from the witch's own body. Although this was part of the vulgar lore of witchcraft that the authorities generally tried to discountenance in 1692, it did have the great advantage of being empirically verifiable, and these documents record a number of physical examinations by surgeons and midwives seeking such preternatural excrescences. Bridget Bishop's body turned up an appendage of this kind ("between the pudendum and Anus much like to Tetts & not usuall in women"—) which provided a further link in the chain of evidence against her.

The weightiness of all this evidence was increased considerably when it was part of a general pattern of proven bad behavior or notorious ill will—when the accused witch already had a poor reputation in the community. Bridget Bishop, for example, had been arrested *before* 1692, not only for witchcraft, but also for the more mundane crime of theft, and, as the testimonies reveal, she had accumulated a large reservoir of hostility over the years. Not even her present husband—the third man to fill this position—came forward to defend her before the Court of Oyer and Terminer. Indeed, it was the cumulative weight of non-spectral evidence against Bishop—the longstanding bad reputation, the instances of anger followed by mischief, the tell-tale puppet, the "witch's tit"—that probably explains why she was singled out to be tried—and hanged—first.

Extracting Confessions

But all of these maddeningly difficult problems of evidence could be solved by a single stroke: a freely given confession. Thus while one object of the preliminary examinations was simply to satisfy the examiners' intense curiosity about witchcraft—What do you use to sign the devil's book? What happens to you when your spirit is out of your body? Do you remember in the morning? etc.—the *central* purpose was to extract a confession. And, literally by the score, confessions *did* pour from the lips of the accused. . . . Indeed, John Hale later claimed that the great number of confessions—about fifty, by his count—was the single factor "which chiefly carried on this matter to such an height. . . ."

These confessions were in large part the product of intense psychological pressure applied during the examination—pressure involving what behavioral psychologists would call both negative and positive reinforcement. As long as the accused person persisted in affirming her innocence, or seemed less than forthright in her answers, the agonies of the afflicted would go on, eventually reaching an almost unbearable intensity. (So great were Mary Warren's torments at the examination of Mary Lacey, Jr., that blood actually ran from her mouth.) But as soon as the suspect *confessed,* not only did the afflicted girls gain relief, but they frequently embraced and tearfully "forgave" their supposed tormenter. Thus to insist on one's innocence came to seem, to the accused herself as well as to the onlookers, an unnatural and heartless act of cruelty, while confession beckoned invitingly as a means both of ending the agonies of the girls and of gaining re-entry—at least for the moment—into the communal fold through an emotional scene of reconciliation.

According to Hale, the confessions were taken with particular seriousness when they were internally consistent, when they confirmed information supplied by the accusers or by other confessing witches, and when they were buttressed by persuasive corroboratory detail. (One such detail has entered the national folklore: a number of confessors reported that they used a pole—not specifically a broomstick, however!—to fly to their witches' meetings.) Abigail Hobbs' confession, for example, goes on almost interminably, piling detail upon detail; and even more persuasive, perhaps, was the confession of Abigail's mother Deliverance Hobbs, for after it was completed her body was examined, and it proved to have two wounds at precisely the same places—one on the right side, one in the left eye—where a young man of Salem Village, at the behest of the afflicted girls, had earlier struck with his sword at her specter!

Confessing Witches Allowed to Live

As it turned out, none of the confessing witches was ever hanged or even brought to trial. As early as May, a decision was made to keep them available to provide testimony against other accused witches who refused to confess—holdouts like Bridget Bishop. (The plan, presumably, was to convict—and execute—the confessors in a group when their testimony was no longer needed.) It was never the intention of the authorities to spare the lives of the confessing witches; that this proved to be the end result was only another of the ironies of 1692.

2

Confessions Elicited in the Jails

Larry Gragg

While confession was considered the best evidence of guilt in witchcraft cases, Larry Gragg explains in this excerpt from *The Salem Witch Crisis* that the available documents suggest that many innocent people confessed in the jails in 1692. Gragg identifies several reasons for these confessions. Some of the accused were harassed into confession by fellow inmates and visitors. Others were pressured into confession during long hours of unrelenting interrogation by magistrates and ministers who came to the jails for the purpose of forcing the accused to confess. Family and friends also urged confession believing that the judges would spare the lives of those who confessed. Some historians believe that the judges granted reprieves for confessing witches, but intended to execute them after they had testified against others; Gragg argues that the judges believed confession was a sign of repentance and therefore a step toward redemption, so the judges probably did not intend to execute repentant witches. Several of the accused died in jail and several more escaped from jail, but most considered confession the safest way to avoid execution, Gragg concludes.

As the judges on the Court of Oyer and Terminer considered further trials, the jailed accused witches struggled with a host of problems. They worried about how their families could continue to pay their escalating jail expenses. Some faced economic ruin because a zealous sheriff and his deputies confiscated their personal property. Conditions in

Excerpted from *The Salem Witch Crisis*, by Larry Gragg (New York: Praeger, 1992). Copyright © 1992 by Larry Gragg. All rights reserved. Reprinted by permission of Greenwood Publishing Group, Inc.

the small, poorly constructed "gaols" were appalling. Worse, magistrates, fellow prisoners, and even kin, with ever greater urgency, tried to convince them to confess. . . .

Pressure from Inmates, Magistrates, Ministers

There was little opportunity for privacy during confinement. In the crowded quarters, some of the accused sought to intimidate new arrivals. Rebecca Eames contended that Abigail Hobbs and Mary Lacey had pressured her into a confession. "Closely confined" with the two women in a Salem jail, Eames said that they mocked her, spat in her face, and repeatedly charged her with witchcraft over the course of four days. Hobbs and Lacey argued that if Eames did not confess, she "should very speedily be hanged." Under the intense grilling, Eames broke down and decided to confess. Besides menacing fellow prisoners, the accused had to endure an almost constant stream of visitors, including the curious and the cruel. Mercy Short, a servant girl on an errand to the Boston jail for her mistress, found Sarah Good intriguing. A pipe smoker, Good asked Short if she would give her some tobacco. The young woman responded by picking up a handful of shavings, tossing them at Good, and taunting her: "That's tobacco good enough for you."

Magistrates and ministers also frequented the jails. They often followed up the examinations with visits to further explore questions that had emerged in the public sessions. More important, they tried to force the accused to confess. Two critics of the magistrates, Thomas Brattle and Robert Calef, offered strikingly similar accounts of the pressures that authorities brought to bear on the accused. Brattle claimed that they faced "violent, distracting, and dragooning methods" and "repeated buzzings and chuckings and unreasonable urgings." Calef agreed, arguing that there were many "tedious" interrogations with questioners "taking turns to persuade them" until "the accused were wearied out by being forced to stand so long, or for want of sleep, etc. and so brought to give an assent to what they said."

There is no mistaking the effectiveness of these techniques. Six women from Andover who confessed to practicing witchcraft later explained that it "was no other than what was suggested to us by some gentlemen; they telling us, that we were witches, and they knew it, and we knew it, and that they knew that we knew it, which made us think that it was so." The relentless grilling, the women claimed, caused them to say "any thing and every thing which they desired, and most of what we said, was but in effect a consenting to what they said." In twenty-year-old Sarah Churchill's case, the authorities "told her they would put her into the dungeon and put her along with Mr. Burroughs." Churchill pointed out that the magistrates and clergymen assumed that an accusation indicated guilt. She explained that "if she told Mr. Noyes but once she had set her hand to the Book he would believe her, but if she told the truth and said she had not set her hand to the Book a hundred times he would not believe her."

As threatening as the interrogations often became, rarely did they include physical torture. A letter of John Proctor's, written from the Salem prison, is the only evidence of such abuse. He described the torture of three young men, including his son William. After rigorous questioning produced no confessions from the three, the jailer "tied them neck and heels till the blood was ready to come out of their noses." Only then, according to Proctor, did Richard and Thomas Carrier confess.

Family and Friends Urge Confession

Jailers and magistrates were not the only ones to prod the accused into a confession. Family and friends, by late summer, were urging the accused to confess. This curious counsel reflected the attitude that the judges on the Court of Oyer and Terminer adopted. Authorities on witchcraft cases had argued that confession was the best evidence of guilt. During the 1692 Salem outbreak, over fifty people confessed to the crime of witchcraft, but the judges chose to spare them. They may have done so to use the confessors to gain evidence about other suspects. The king's attorney Thomas Newton recommended that approach in the case of two of the accused in late May. He asked that "Tituba the Indian & Mrs. Thatcher's maid may be transferred as evidences but desire they may not come amongst the prisoners but rather by themselves." Newton may have intended to delay prosecution of the confessors only as long as they were useful. Paul Boyer and Stephen Nissenbaum believe that the judges ultimately planned to execute "the confessors in a group when their testimony was no longer needed." Yet the judges' actions suggest another explanation. They seemed to believe that a confession served as the first step toward redemption. For example, when they confronted Mary Lacey, Jr., they said, "You are now in the way to obtain mercy if you will confess and repent. . . . Do not you desire to be saved by Christ?" Her answer: "Yes." "Then you must confess freely what you know in this matter." Similarly, they told John Willard, "If you can therefore find in your heart to repent, it is possible you may obtain mercy."

Besides menacing fellow prisoners, the accused had to endure an almost constant stream of visitors, including the curious and the cruel.

The best measure of the judges' intent is in their actions. Dorcas Hoar, with five others, was convicted on September 9. The judges scheduled their execution for September 22. On September 21, Hoar, who had proclaimed her innocence all along, confessed to four clergymen who petitioned the judges for a delay in her execution. The ministers explained that Hoar, "out of distress of conscience," had confessed to the crime and had told them "how & when she was taken in the snare of the Devil." The penitent woman now sought "a little longer time of life to realize & perfect her repentance for the salvation of her soul." On Hoar's behalf, the clergymen requested "one month's time or more to prepare for death & eternity." Not only would the postponement give her the opportunity to discover "these mysteries of iniquity" but also it might encourage "others to confess & give glory to God." The judges obliged and ordered "that her execution be respited until further order." The hope they had expressed in the cases of Mary Lacey, Jr., and John Willard had been realized. For Judge Samuel Sewall, Hoar's confession represented a significant breakthrough. Although he made few references to the witchcraft in his diary, on September 21 Sewall noted the order "sent to the sheriff to forbear her execution, notwithstanding her being in the warrant to die tomorrow. This is the first condemned person who has confessed." Whether the judges would have eventually permitted Hoar's execution had not Governor Phips ordered a halt to the trials is unclear. Families of the accused saw little ambiguity, however, in the words and deeds of the judges. The best way to save kin was to convince them to confess. Six confessed witches from Andover admitted as much: "Our nearest and dearest relations . . . apprehending that there was no other way to save our lives . . . but by our confessing . . . they out of tender love and pity persuaded us to confess what we did confess."

When Increase Mather visited Martha Tyler in prison, he discovered how even an individual who believed that "nothing could have made her confess against herself" could be persuaded by a brother to do so. Tyler told Mather that her brother Bridges rode with her when authorities took her from Andover to Salem to be examined. "All along the way," he "kept telling her she must needs be a witch" since the afflicted had accused her and "at her touch were raised out of their fits." Martha told him repeatedly that she was not a witch and "knew nothing of witchcraft." When they finally arrived in Salem, Tyler found herself in a room with her brother and Charlestown schoolmaster John Emerson. The two men continued the effort to persuade her to confess. They even told Martha what to say, that "she was certainly a witch, and . . . she saw the Devil before her eyes at that time (and, accordingly, they said Emerson would attempt with his hand to beat him away from her eyes)." Their entreaties became so intense, Tyler told Mather, that she "wished herself in any dungeon, rather than be so treated." When Emerson gave up, he told Tyler, "Well, I see you will not confess! . . . then you are undone, body and soul, for ever."

[The judges] seemed to believe that a confession served as the first step toward redemption.

Bridges Tyler persisted. He told his sister, "God would not suffer so many good men to be in such an error about it." Apparently no argument would work with her. She protested to her brother, "I shall lie if I confess, and then who shall answer unto God for my lie?" After trying to persuade his sister that she must be a witch because of the actions of the afflicted and the magistrates, Bridges finally explained to her his real reason for demanding that she confess. It was simply that "she would be hanged if she did not confess."

Because of her arrest, trip under guard to Salem, and the prolonged harangue of her brother, Martha Tyler "became so terrified in her mind that she owned . . . almost any thing that they propounded to her." When she appeared before the magistrates on September 17, Martha confessed to practicing witchcraft. However, when Increase Mather saw her in jail afterward, he found a woman suffering from profound guilt for "belying of herself" to save her life. The minister saw in her so much "affection, sorrow, relenting, grief, and mourning, as it exceeds any pen to describe."

Jail Conditions Deplorable for Most

The conditions of their incarceration broke the health or spirit of many. Several prisoners and their families complained about the conditions of the jails and the treatment from jailers. Their kin were "dangerously sick"; they suffered "inward grief and trouble." After several months in jail, ten prisoners from Ipswich claimed, "Some of us being aged either about or near four score some though younger yet being with child, and one giving suck to a child not ten weeks old yet, and all of us weak and infirm at the best, and one fettered with irons this half year and all most destroyed with so long an imprisonment." Nicholas Rice explained to the General Court in late October that his wife, Sarah, had "lain in Boston gaol" since June 1. "It is deplorable," he wrote, "that in old age the poor decrepit woman should lie under confinement so long in a stinking gaol when her circumstances rather requires a nurse to attend her." Elizabeth Cary suffered terribly almost from the moment of her incarceration. Her husband later explained that within a day, the jailer put her into leg irons. "These irons and her other afflictions," he wrote, "soon brought her into convulsion fits, so that I thought she would have died that night." He pleaded for the removal of the eight-pound irons, "but all entreaties were in vain."

Some did not survive the wretched conditions. Already ill when she entered jail, Sarah Osborne lingered for a couple of months before dying on May 10. Jailed on May 18, Roger Toothaker, a physician from Billerica, lasted less than one month of incarceration. However, on June 16, a Suffolk County coroner's jury ruled that Toothaker "came to his end by a natural death." Though convicted on September 17, Ann Foster, an old woman from Andover, escaped the executioner because of her confession. She remained in jail for over five months and died in December.

Sarah Good, jailed in early March, had a baby apparently on April 5 because the Boston jailer noted in his account book, "2 blankets for Sarah Good's child." The infant died before its mother's execution on July 19.

Prison for people of property and standing, like all of life in the seventeenth century, was less traumatic than for most of the accused. Merchant Philip English and his wife, Mary, for example, enjoyed liberties "suitable to their station." Their jailer permitted them to leave to attend worship services as long as they returned in the evening. In early August, the couple heard a sermon with an unmistakable message by Joshua Moody. A critic of the trials, Moody based his sermon on Matthew 10:23: "If they persecute you in one city, flee to another." The clergyman, joined by Samuel Willard, who had also become an opponent of the trials, accompanied English and his wife back to their prison and urged them to take the sermon text literally. Although English argued that God would "not permit them to touch me," he relented and agreed to flee. With a carriage provided by Boston merchants and a letter of introduction from Governor Phips, Philip and Mary English escaped to New York where Governor Benjamin Fletcher gave them sanctuary.

Surprisingly, only a dozen other accused witches also tried to escape. . . .

Confession to Avoid Execution

Some who stayed behind did so because they knew that they were innocent and believed that they would be vindicated. As Philip English had proclaimed, before being convinced otherwise, "God will not permit them to touch me." Others felt helpless, overwhelmed by the frightening circumstances facing them. If eight Andover petitioners accurately described the situation in October, many in Salem area jails were "a company of poor distressed creatures as full of inward grief and trouble as they are able to bear up in life withall and besides that the aggravation of outward troubles and hardships they undergo." Some believed that running would send the wrong message about their innocence. As magistrates John Hathorne and Jonathan Corwin explained to the captured John Willard, fleeing from arrest "is acknowledgment of guilt." Most important, as the summer wore on, escape became less attractive as it became ever clearer that confession afforded a safer way to avoid execution.

3

A Word of Caution About the Validity of Confessions

Mary Easty

Mary Easty was arrested for witchcraft in April of 1692, condemned on September 9, and executed on September 22. Her sister, Rebecca Nurse, was hanged as a witch on July 19, and her other sister, Sarah Cloyce, was arrested and imprisoned but eventually cleared in January of 1693.

In a petition to Governor Phips before her execution, Mary Easty proclaimed her innocence and urged Phips to separate and closely examine the afflicted girls who were the chief accusers; she also urged Phips to question the confessing witches. Mary Easty's moving appeal reveals her clear understanding of her own position; it also counsels caution about accepting the testimony of both the afflicted girls and the confessing witches.

The humbl petition of mary Eastick [Easty] unto his Excellencyes S'r W'm Phipps to the honour'd Judge and Bench now Sitting In Judicature in Salem and the Reverend ministers humbly sheweth

That whereas your poor and humble Petition being condemned to die Doe humbly begg of you to take it into your Judicious and pious considerations that your Poor and humble petitioner knowing my own Innocencye Blised be the Lord for it and seeing plainly the wiles and subtility of my accusers by my Selfe can not but Judg charitably of oth-

Excerpted from "The Petition of Mary Easty," by Mary Easty, *Essex County Archives*, September 1692.

ers that are going the same way of my selfe if the Lord
stepps not mightily in i was confined a whole month upon
the same account that I am condemed now for and then
cleared by the afflicted persons as some of your honours
know and in two dayes time I was cryed out upon by them
and have been confined and now am condemned to die the
Lord above knows my Innocencye then and Likewise does
now as att the great day will be known to men and Angells—
I Petition to your honours not for my own life for I know I
must die and my appointed time is sett but the Lord he
knowes it is that if it be possible no more Innocentt blood
may be shed which undoubtidly cannot be Avoydd In the
way and course you goe in I question not but your honours
does to the uttmost of your Powers in the discovery and de-
tecting of witchcraft and witches and would not be gulty of
Innocent blood for the world but by my own Innocencye I
know you are in the wrong way the Lord in his infinite mer-
cye direct you in this great work if it be his blessed will that
no more Innocent blood be shed I would humbly begg of
you that your honors would be plesed to examine theis
Aflicted Persons strictly and keepe them apart some time
and Likewise to try some of these confesing wichis I being
confident there is severall of them has belyed themselves
and others as will appeare if not in this wor[l]d I am sure in
the world to come whither I am now agoing and I Question
not but youle see an alteration of thes things they say my
selfe and others having made a League with the Divel we
cannot confesse I know and the Lord knowes as will shortly
appeare they belye me and so I Question not but they doe
others the Lord above who is the Searcher of all hearts
knowes that as I shall answer it att the Tribunall seat that I
know not the least thinge of witchcraft therfore I cannot I
dare not belye my own soule I beg your honers not to deny
this my humble petition from a poor dying Innocent person
and I Question not but the Lord will give a blesing to yor
endevers

4

The Use of Torture to Elicit Confessions

John Proctor

Physical torture does not appear to have been commonly used to elicit confessions or to encourage accusations of others, but John Proctor, who was arrested for witchcraft in April 1692, condemned on August 5 and executed August 19, insisted that torture was used on his son and on two of Martha Carrier's sons. (Martha Carrier was arrested in May 1692, condemned August 5, and executed August 19.)

In this letter written from Salem prison July 23, 1692, John Proctor comments on five prisoners who had recently confessed in jail. He claims that Martha Carrier's two sons had only confessed after being tied "Neck and Heel." The same cruel treatment did not result in a confession from Proctor's son, who insisted on his innocence and was eventually unbound.

(Petition of John Proctor)

SALEM-PRISON, July 23, 1692.

Mr. [Increase] Mather, Mr. [James] Allen,
Mr. [Joshua] Moody, Mr. [Samuel] Willard, and
Mr. [John] Bailey.
Reverend Gentlemen. [all of the above are ministers]

The innocency of our Case with the Enmity of our Accusers and our Judges, and Jury, whom nothing but our Innocent Blood will serve their turn, having Condemned us

From "The Petition of John Proctor," by John Proctor, *More Wonders of the Invisible World*, edited by Robert Calef (London, 1700).

already before our Tryals, being so much incensed and engaged against us by the Devil, makes us bold to Beg and Implore your Favourable Assistance of this our Humble Petition to his Excellency, That if it be possible our Innocent Blood may be spared, which undoubtedly otherwise will be shed, if the Lord doth not mercifully step in. The Magistrates, Ministers, Jewries, and all the People in general, being so much inraged and incensed against us by the Delusion of the Devil, which we can term no other, by reason we know in our own Consciences, we are all Innocent Persons. Here are five Persons who have lately confessed themselves to be Witches, and do accuse some of us, of being along with them at a Sacrament, since we were committed into close Prison, which we know to be Lies. Two of the 5 are ([Martha] Carriers Sons [Richard and Andrew]) Youngmen, who would not confess any thing till they tyed them Neck and Heels till the Blood was ready to come out of their Noses, and 'tis credibly believed and reported this was the occasion of making them confess that they never did, by reason they said one had been a Witch a Month, and another five Weeks, and that their Mother had made them so, who has been confined here this nine Weeks. My son William Procter, when he was examin'd, because he would not confess that he was Guilty, when he was Innocent, they tyed him Neck and Heels till the Blood gushed out at his Nose, and would have kept him so 24 Hours, if one more Merciful than the rest, had not taken pity on him, and caused him to be unbound. These actions are very like the Popish Cruelties. They have already undone us in our Estates, and that will not serve their turns, without our Innocent Bloods. If it cannot be granted that we can have our Trials at Boston, we humbly beg that you would endeavor to have these Magistrates changed, and others in their rooms, begging also and beseeching you would be pleased to be here, if not all, some of you at our Trials, hoping thereby you may be the means of saving the shedding our Innocent Bloods, desiring your Prayers to the Lord in our behalf, we rest your Poor Afflicted Servants,

JOHN PROCTER, etc.

5

Giles Corey's Silent Indictment of the Court

David C. Brown

By mid-September 1692 it had become clear that accused witches who refused to confess would be executed. Twenty-seven trials had resulted in twenty-seven convictions. One convicted woman escaped; two pregnant women and five women who confessed were reprieved. Nineteen women and men who refused to confess and who vocally maintained their innocence to the end were hanged for witchcraft; one eighty-one-year-old man, Giles Corey, was pressed to death for "standing mute."

Historians commonly report that Corey had refused to plead either guilty or not guilty (perhaps to avoid forfeiture of his sizable property) and that the court's decision to use *peine forte et dure* (hard and severe punishment) was an effort to force him to enter a plea so that he could be tried before a jury. However, David C. Brown contends that Corey did in fact plead not guilty and that he did not fear forfeiture of his property, since such forfeiture was illegal in witchcraft cases. "Standing mute," Brown argues, meant that Corey refused to stand trial after entering his plea. Brown believes that Corey refused to stand trial because he felt contempt for a court that appeared to have predetermined his guilt.

The case of Giles Corey, who was pressed to death in Salem in 1692, is one of the most intriguing cases of the Salem witchcraft trials. It is also one of the most remarkable episodes in the entire history of American ju-

Excerpted from "The Case of Giles Cory," by David C. Brown, *Essex Institute Historical Collections*, October 1985. Copyright © 1985 by Essex Institute Historical Collections. Reprinted with permission.

risprudence, yet historians since the nineteenth century have consistently distorted the facts of his case. The prevailing view holds that he resolutely refused to plead to the indictments brought against him, and endured the *peine forte et dure* rather than risk the forfeiture of his estate that would have resulted from his conviction. That view has prevailed in no small part because historians have failed to understand the legal complexities that bear on Corey's case. It is totally incorrect.

This article will attempt to set the record straight. It will conclusively show first, that Giles Corey pleaded "not guilty" to his indictment, but was pressed to death because he would not "put himself on the country," that is, submit to trial by jury; second, that whatever Corey's motive for "standing mute," fear of forfeiture was not a part of it because forfeiture of one's estate upon conviction for witchcraft was illegal both in Massachusetts and in England; and third, that the *peine forte et dure*, to which Corey was subjected in 1692, was not only illegal in Massachusetts, but was only one of a number of illegal acts performed by the Massachusetts authorities during the Salem witchcraft trials.

Corey's Arrest and Examination

Giles Corey was eighty-one years old in 1692 and lived on a farm of over one hundred acres located off what is now Pine Street in West Peabody. His wife, Martha, had been arrested, examined, and imprisoned on suspicion of witchcraft in March 1692. In April it was Giles's turn. On 18 April, a warrant was sworn out for his arrest together with the arrests of Mary Warren, Abigail Hobbs, and Bridget Bishop:

> for high Suspition of Sundry acts of Witchcraft donne or Committed by them, upon the Bodys of: Ann Putnam, Marcy Lewis, and Abig'l Williams and Mary Walcot and Eliz. Hubert—of Salem village—whereby great hurt and damage hath benne donne to the Bodys of Said persons above named.

The following day, Corey was examined by John Hathorne and Jonathan Corwin in Salem Village. The girls accused him of grievously afflicting them; but Corey maintained his innocence. He protested that "I never had no hand in [witchcraft], in my life." After his examination he was imprisoned first in Salem and later in Ipswich gaol awaiting trial.

While in prison in Ipswich, Corey drew up a deed conveying his property to two of his sons-in-law, William Cleeves of Beverly and John Moulton of Salem. In it Corey wrote that he lay "under great trouble and affliction" and knew "not how soon I may depart this life." He had good reason to be afraid. Between June and August 1692, the infamous Court of Oyer and Terminer sat three separate times in Salem. At these sittings, twelve people were tried for witchcraft and condemned, of which all save one, Elizabeth Proctor, had been executed. . . .

Corey's Plea

Sometime after 9 September (the records do not indicate exactly when), Corey was brought to trial before the petty jury of the Court of Oyer and Terminer. According to Robert Calef, who gives the most detailed account of the event:

> Giles Cory pleaded not Guilty to his Indictment, but would not put himself upon Tryal by the Jury (they having cleared none upon Tryal) and knowing there would be the same Witnesses against him, rather chose to undergo what Death they would put him to.

Other contemporaries give the story somewhat differently. Nicholas Noyes and Cotton Mather wrote that Corey refused to plead; whereas Thomas Brattle and Samuel Sewall both wrote that Corey stood "mute" before the court. The weight of available evidence supports Calef's account. Both Sewall's and Brattle's accounts, as we will see, are entirely compatible with Calef's version; and the accounts given by Noyes and Mather are sketchy and most likely represent a simplification of what actually occurred.

"Standing Mute"

Legal procedures have changed considerably since the seventeenth century. Under seventeenth-century English law, a defendant could not be tried for any crime unless he pleaded to his indictment, and if he pleaded "not guilty," submitted himself to trial by the petit jury. After pleading "not guilty," the court would ask the defendant, "Culprit, how will you be tried?" to which he was required to answer "By God and my country." The phrase "by God and my country" was sacrosanct, and had to be said in its entirety—answering either "by God" or "by my country" alone did not suffice—before the defendant could be tried. Saying this phrase was known legally as "putting oneself on the country"; and it is this phrase that Giles Corey refused to say.

The history of the phrase "by God and my country," is itself very interesting. In the early middle ages, English trials were based on the ordeal, in which the defendant was required to perform a miraculous feat to prove his innocence. This was grounded in the belief that God would always intervene to acquit an innocent man and grant him the power to perform the required feat. Trial by a jury of one's peers came later and was, at first, an exceptional privilege; so exceptional, in fact, that initially the defendant paid money to the king in order to exercise it. At some point in the history of English law, the defendant no doubt answered the question "Culprit, how will you be tried?" by saying "by God" if he intended to undergo the ordeal or "by my country" if he chose a trial by jury. After 1215, when the ordeal was abolished, its vestiges nevertheless persisted in the inclusive phrase "by God and my country." And because defendants had historically requested jury trial, they could not be tried until they requested it from the authorities by "putting themselves on the country."

[Corey] protested that "I never had no hand in [witchcraft], in my life."

There is no doubt that the requirement that the defendant "put himself on the country" was strictly adhered to by the Court of Oyer and Terminer in Salem in 1692. Although the records of the proceedings of that infamous court have disappeared, accessory documents shed light on the manner in which its victims placed themselves on trial. Bridget Bishop's death warrant, for example, which was signed by Chief Justice William Stoughton himself on 8 June, states that she "pleaded not guilty and for Tryall thereof put her selfe upon God and her Country." Similar words are to be found in the death warrant for the five women hanged on 19 July and in the records of the witchcraft cases tried before the Superior Court of Judicature in 1693.

Giles Corey's refusal to "put himself on the country" was known as "standing mute" in the seventeenth century. According to Blackstone:

. . . a prisoner is said to stand mute when, being arraigned for treason or felony, he either, 1. Makes no answer at all; 2. Answers foreign to the purpose, or with such matter as is not allowable; and will not answer otherwise; or, 3. Upon having pleaded not guilty refuses to put himself upon the country.

Clearly, Corey "stood mute" because he violated Blackstone's third tenet. . . .

Peine Forte et Dure

The nature of the offense with which the defendant was charged determined how the court dealt with prisoners who either "stood mute" of malice or refused to "put themselves on the country." If the prisoner was charged with high treason, petty larceny, or a misdemeanor, standing mute was equivalent to conviction. But in cases of petty treason or felony (and under English law, witchcraft was considered a felony), the ancient laws of England did not

Giles Corey maintained his innocence, refusing to stand trial for witchcraft. As a result, he was pressed to death.

equate standing mute with conviction; and since the defendant could not be tried if he "stood mute" of malice or refused to "put himself on the country," these prisoners instead received the dread sentence of the *peine forte et dure* [hard and severe punishment].

Before this sentence was passed, however, "the prisoner had not only *trina admonitio* [three warnings], but also a respite of a few hours, and the sentence was distinctly read to him, that he might know his danger." If he persisted in standing mute after these warnings, however, the sentence was pronounced. According to Blackstone, the prisoner was then:

> . . . remanded to the prison from whence he came, and put into a low, dark chamber, and thereby laid on his back on the bare floor, naked, unless where decency forbids; that there be placed upon his body as great a weight of iron as he could bear, and more; that he have no sustenance, save only, on the first day, three morsels of the worst bread; and, on the second day, three draughts of standing water, that should be nearest to the prison-door; and in this situation this should be alternately his daily diet *till he died*, or (as anciently the judgment ran) *till he answered.*

Barrington adds that, on occasion, a sharp stone was placed beneath the victim's back, and that the prisoner would often be staked to the ground with ropes extending his limbs "as far as they could be stretched."

The history of the *peine forte et dure* provides another example of the evolution of English law. Originally, the law provided that prisoners charged with felony or petty treason who "stood mute" were to be subjected to *prisone forte et dure* which consisted of "a very strait confinement in prison, with hardly any degree of sustenance." The prisoner was thus confined until he either pleaded (or, depending on the circumstances, "put himself on the country") or died. The English laws do not mention pressing at all, initially. Rather it appears that pressing was a later innovation. The itinerant justices of Eyre and justices of gaol-delivery, who traveled around the country and tried the cases brought before them in each town, could afford to remain in each town for only a few days. A prisoner who "stood mute," however, could endure the *prisone forte et dure* for weeks and delay the justices' work indeterminately. So pressing was gradually introduced between the statutes of 31 Edw. III. and 8 Hen. IV., at which point it finally became law. No prisoner could survive the *peine forte et dure* for days on end; and the justices could again go about their work on schedule. . . .

Corey Is Pressed to Death

No one will ever know exactly what happened to Giles Corey in September 1692. It appears that the court gave him the required three warnings, for in a letter written by Thomas Putnam to Samuel Sewall on 19 September, Putnam wrote that Corey was "often before the Court." If the English laws were strictly followed, after the sentence was passed, Corey would have been taken to the Salem gaol and pressed there. Tradition has it, however, that he was executed in an open field near the gaol and that, seeking to hasten his death, he pleaded for "more weight" from the authorities. Calef describes his last moments: "In pressing his Tongue being prest out of his Mouth, the Sheriff with his Cane forced it in again, when he was dying."

No one is even sure how long Corey was subjected to the *peine forte et dure*. Calef wrote that Corey was pressed to death on 16 September; but Judge Sewall, under his diary entry for 19 September 1692, has written:

> About noon, at Salem, Giles Corey was press'd to death for standing Mute; much pains was used with him two days, one after another, by the Court and Capt. Gardner of Nantucket who had been of his acquaintance: but all in vain. . . .

Property Seizure Illegal

Almost every historian of the Salem witchcraft has attributed Corey's refusal to stand trial to his fear that, upon conviction of the felony of witchcraft, his entire estate would be forfeited. The laws of both Massachusetts and England in 1692, however, forbade forfeitures after conviction for witchcraft. Unless someone cruelly deceived Giles Corey into believing that, contrary to law, his property would be forfeited upon his conviction, the preceding historical myth is completely untenable.

In 1641 the famous Body of Liberties, which protected the rights of the colony's inhabitants, was drawn up by

Nathaniel Ward of Ipswich and was adopted by the General Court. Two of its articles are relevant to the question of forfeiture:

> 1. . . . no mans goods or estaite shall be taken away from him, nor any way indammaged under coulor of law or Countenance of Authoritie, unlesse it be by vertue or equitie of some expresse law of the Country waranting the same, established by a generall Court and sufficiently published, or in case of the defect of a law in any parteculer case by the word of god.

> 10. All our lands and heritages shall be free from all fines and licences upon Alienations, and from all hariotts, wardships, Liveries, Primer-seisins, yeare day and wast, Escheates, and forfeitures, upon the deaths of parents or Ancestors, be they naturall, casuall or Juditiall. . . .

On 15 June 1692 the General Court passed the act continuing all the Massachusetts laws passed under the colony governments that were "not repugnant to the laws of England." In this manner, the Body of Liberties of 1641 continued as recognized law of the land; and the forfeiture of goods, chattels, lands, or heritages upon conviction for witchcraft was illegal. These provisions were not tampered with until 13 October 1692, almost a month after Corey's death, when the General Court passed "An Act Setting Forth General Privileges" which provided in part that:

> All lands and heritages within this province shall be free from year, day and wast, escheats and forfeitures, upon the death of parents or ancestors, natural, casual or judicial, and that for ever, except in cases of high treason.

This provision is essentially identical to Article 10 of the 1641 Body of Liberties except that forfeiture was now permitted in cases of high treason (but not felony) . . . .

Peine Forte et Dure Illegal

The history of Massachusetts records only one other case in which a prisoner was threatened with the *peine forte et dure*. In the winter of 1638-39, Dorothy Talbye, a onetime member of the Salem church, was indicted for murdering her three-year-old daughter; and although she confessed to the crime at her arrest, Gov. John Winthrop recorded in his

History that "at her arraignment, she stood mute a good space, till the governour [Winthrop himself] told her she should be pressed to death, and then she confessed the indictment" and was later hanged.

Pressing was one of the cruelest punishments ever devised.

Two years later, cruel and unusual punishment was abolished by the Body of Liberties: "For bodilie punishments we allow amongst us none that are inhumane Barbarous or cruel." In 1692 this abolition was confirmed, when on 15 June the General Court passed the bill continuing all the colony laws that were not repugnant to the laws of England. Thus the *peine forte et dure* was illegal in Massachusetts for two reasons: first, there was no express law of the province permitting pressing; and second, because it violated the provisions of the Body of Liberties regarding barbarous punishments. Pressing was one of the cruelest punishments ever devised and it is a stark testimony to its cruelty that so few felons "stood mute" and chose to endure the horrible *peine forte et dure* rather than stand trial. By Massachusetts law, Corey's punishment was illegal. It was borrowed from the English legal tradition to coerce this poor but obstinate prisoner to put himself on the country. Calef, who noted the strange use of this English punishment, wrote that "the Executions seemed mixt, in pressing to death for not pleading, which most agrees with the Laws of England."

Corey's Silence Condemns the Court

Why then did Giles Corey "stand mute" in September 1692 when he was brought to trial before the Court of Oyer and Terminer? Calef, who gives the fullest account of the event, relates that Corey:

> . . . would not put himself upon Tryal by the Jury (they having cleared none upon Tryal) and knowing there would be the same Witnesses against him, rather chose to undergo what Death they would put him to.

The Court of Oyer and Terminer that summer had failed to acquit anyone accused of witchcraft; and the magistrates at Corey's examination in April and the jury of inquest that considered his case on 9 September had willingly believed the same witnesses who were to appear at his trial. No doubt Corey felt that if he were tried, his conviction was a foregone conclusion. When he was brought before the court, he pleaded "Not guilty" to his indictment and thus maintained his innocence; but to the question, "Culprit, how will you be tried?" he "stood mute" and would not answer "by God and my country." He thus refused to submit himself to the jurisdiction of a court which had predetermined his guilt, and he showed his contempt for that court by suffering the *peine forte et dure* rather than by standing trial.

6

Judge Samuel Sewall Confesses Shame and Guilt

Samuel Sewall

Samuel Sewall is best known today for writing the first anti-slavery tract in America, "The Selling of Joseph," and *The Diary of Samuel Sewall*, which begins December 3, 1673, and ends on December 25, 1728. He was one of the seven councillors appointed by Governor William Phips to the Court of Oyer and Terminer which condemned twenty-seven people as witches and executed nineteen of them in 1692. In addition Sewall was appointed to the Superior Court of Judicature which acquitted forty-nine confessing witches in the early months of 1693.

In the following extracts from his *Diary*, Sewall comments briefly on those condemned and executed in 1692. The 1697 entry records the Bill which Sewall requested be read from the pulpit on January 14. Samuel Sewall was the only judge to make a public statement about his culpability in the Salem witch trials. Sewall's confession may have been prompted by the deaths of two of his children in 1696, tragedies he attributed to an angry God.

April 11th 1692. Went to Salem, where, in the Meeting-house, the persons accused of Witchcraft were examined; was a very great Assembly; 'twas awfull to see how the afflicted persons were agitated. Mr. Noyes pray'd at the beginning, and Mr. Higginson concluded. [*In the margin*], Vae, Vae, Vae, Witchcraft [Woe, Woe, Woe, Witchcraft].

Excerpted from *The Diary of Samuel Sewall*, edited by M. Halsey Thomas (New York: Farrar, Straus, & Giroux, 1973). Copyright © 1973 by Farrar, Straus, & Giroux. Reprinted with permission.

July 30, 1692. Mrs. Cary makes her escape out of Cambridge-Prison, who was Committed for Witchcraft [Elizabeth Cary fled to New York].

Augt. 4. [1692] At Salem, Mr. Waterhouse brings the news of the desolation at Jamaica, June 7th. 1700 persons kill'd, besides the Loss of Houses and Goods by the Earthquake.

Augt. 19th 1692 . . . This day [*in the margin*, Dolefull Witchcraft] George Burrough, John Willard, Jn Procter, Martha Carrier and George Jacobs were executed at Salem, a very great number of Spectators being present. Mr. Cotton Mather was there, Mr. Sims, [Rev. John] Hale, [Rev. Nicholas] Noyes, [Rev. Samuel] Chiever, &c. All of them said they were innocent, Carrier and all. Mr. Mather says they all died by a Righteous Sentence. Mr. [George] Burrough by his Speech, Prayer, protestation of his Innocence, did much move unthinking persons, which occasions their speaking hardly concerning his being executed.

Augt. 25. [1692] Fast at the old [First] Church, respecting the Witchcraft, Drought, &c.

Monday, Sept. 19, 1692. About noon, at Salem, Giles Corey was press'd to death for standing Mute; much pains was used with him two days, one after another, by the Court and Capt. Gardner of Nantucket who had been of his acquaintance: but all in vain.

Sept. 20. [1692] Now I hear from Salem that about 18 years agoe, he was suspected to have stamped and press'd a man to death, but was cleared. Twas not remembred till Anne Putnam was told of it by said Corey's Spectre the Sabbath-day night before Execution.

Sept. 20, 1692. The Swan brings in a rich French Prize of about 300 Tuns, laden with Claret, White Wine, Brandy, Salt, Linnen Paper, &c.

Sept. 21. [1692] A petition is sent to Town in behalf of Dorcas Hoar, who now confesses: Accordingly an order is sent to the Sheriff to forbear her Execution, notwithstanding her being in the Warrant to die to morrow. This is the first condemned person who has confess'd.

Nov. 6. [1692] Joseph [Sewall's son] threw a knop of Brass and hit his Sister Betty on the forhead so as to make it bleed and swell; upon which, and for his playing at Prayer-time, and eating when Return Thanks, I whipd him pretty smartly. When I first went in (call'd by his Grandmother) he sought to shadow and hide himself from me behind the head of the Cradle: which gave me the sorrowfull remembrance of Adam's carriage.

Monday, April 29, 1695. The morning is very warm and Sunshiny; in the Afternoon there is Thunder and Lightening, and about 2 P.M. a very extraordinary Storm of Hail, so that the ground was made white with it, as with the blossoms when fallen; 'twas as bigg as pistoll and Musquet Bullets; It broke of the Glass of the new House about 480 Quarrels [squares] of the Front; of Mr. Sergeant's about as much; Col. Shrimpton, Major General, Govr Bradstreet, New Meetinghouse, Mr. Willard, &c. Mr. Cotton Mather dined with us, and was with me in the new Kitchen when this was; He had just been mentioning that more Minister Houses than others proportionably had been smitten with Lightening; enquiring what the meaning of God should be in it. Many Hail-Stones broke threw the Glass and flew to the middle of the Room, or farther: People afterward Gazed upon the House to see its Ruins. I got Mr. Mather to pray with us after this awfull Providence; He told God He had broken the brittle part of our house, and prayd that we might be ready for the time when our Clay-Tabernacles should be broken. 'Twas a sorrowfull thing to me to see the house so far undon again before twas finish'd. It seems at Milton [near Boston] on the one hand, and at Lewis's [the tavern at Lynn] on the other, there was no Hail.

Jany 15. [1697] . . . Copy of the Bill I put up on the Fast day [January 14]; giving it to Mr. Willard as he pass'd by, and standing up at the reading of it, and bowing when finished; in the Afternoon.

Samuel Sewall, sensible of the reiterated strokes of God upon himself and family, and being sensible, that as to the Guilt contracted, upon the opening of the late Commission of Oyer and Terminer at Salem (to which the order for this Day relates) he is, upon many accounts, more concerned than any that he knows of, Desires to take the Blame and Shame of it, Asking pardon of Men, And especially desiring prayers that God, who has an Unlimited Authority, would pardon that Sin and all other his Sins; personal and Relative: And according to his infinite Benignity, and Soveraignty, Not Visit the Sin of him, or of any other, upon himself or any of his, nor upon the Land: But that He would powerfully defend him against all Temptations to Sin, for the future; and vouchsafe him the Efficacious, Saving Conduct of his Word and Spirit.

List of the Accusers and the Accused

The "Afflicted" Girls

- 9-year-old Elizabeth (Betty) Parris, daughter of Reverend Samuel Parris
- 11-year-old Abigail Williams, niece of Reverend Samuel Parris
- 17-year-old Elizabeth Hubbard, niece of Dr. Griggs's wife and a servant in the Griggs's home
- 12-year-old Ann Putnam, daughter of Thomas and Ann Carr Putnam
- 17-year-old Mary Walcott, niece of the Putnams
- 17-year-old Mercy Lewis, servant in the Putnam home
- 30-year-old Ann Carr Putnam, mother of 12-year-old Ann
- 20-year-old Sarah Churchill, servant of George Jacobs
- 20-year-old Mary Warren, servant of John Proctor
- 18-year-old Susannah Sheldon
- 18-year-old Elizabeth Booth

Partial List of Those Arrested for Witchcraft in 1692

- Sarah Good and infant child, Sarah Osborne, and Tituba (February 29); the infant and Sarah Osborne later die in prison
- Martha Corey (March 19)
- Rebecca Nurse and four-year-old Dorcas Good (daughter of Sarah Good) (March 23)
- Sarah Cloyce (sister of Rebecca Nurse) and Elizabeth Proctor (April 4)
- John Proctor (April 11)
- Giles Corey, Bridget Bishop, Abigail Hobbs, and Mary Warren (April 18); Warren is soon released as one of the "afflicted" girls
- William Hobbs, Deliverance Hobbs, Mary Easty (sister of Rebecca Nurse), Edward Bishop, Sarah Bishop, Sarah Wildes, and Mary English (April 21)
- Philip English, Lydia Dustin, Susannah Martin, Dorcas Hoar, Sarah Morrell, and Reverend George Burroughs (April 30)

- George Jacobs, Margaret Jacobs, and John Willard (May 10)
- Alice Parker and Ann Pudeator (May 12)
- Dr. Roger Toothaker (May 18); Toothaker later dies in prison
- William Proctor, Elizabeth Howe, Martha Carrier, Elizabeth Cary, John Alden, Wilmot Reed, and Mary Toothaker (May 28)
- Sarah Churchill (June 1); soon released as one of the "afflicted" girls
- Mary Bradbury (June 28)
- Ann Foster (July 15); Foster dies in prison after being reprieved
- Mary Lacey (July 19)
- Richard and Andrew Carrier (July 21)
- Margaret Scott (August 5)
- Abigail Faulkner (August 11)
- Samuel Wardwell (August 15)
- Rebecca Eames (August 21)
- Mary Parker (September 1)

Of the 27 who were tried and convicted, 7 were given reprieves for confession or pregnancy, 1 escaped from jail, and 19 were hanged.

Those Executed by Order of the Court of Oyer and Terminer in 1692

1. Bridget Bishop—hanged June 10
2. Sarah Good—hanged July 19
3. Sarah Wildes—hanged July 19
4. Rebecca Nurse—hanged July 19
5. Susannah Martin—hanged July 19
6. Elizabeth Howe—hanged July 19
7. Martha Carrier—hanged August 19
8. John Proctor—hanged August 19
9. Reverend George Burroughs—hanged August 19
10. John Willard—hanged August 19
11. George Jacobs—hanged August 19
12. Martha Corey—hanged September 22
13. Mary Easty—hanged September 22
14. Alice Parker—hanged September 22
15. Ann Pudeator—hanged September 22
16. Wilmot Reed—hanged September 22
17. Margaret Scott—hanged September 22
18. Samuel Wardwell—hanged September 22
19. Mary Parker—hanged September 22
20. Giles Corey—pressed to death September 19

Chronology

1626

Salem Town was settled in 1626 as a fishing station, but the colony was chartered in 1629.

1630s

Settlement begins in the "Salem Farms" region of town.

1638

Jane Hawkins, suspected witch, is banished from Massachusetts.

1647

Alice Young is the first to be executed for witchcraft in New England.

1662

Hartford, Connecticut witch-hunt: eight are accused, and four are executed.

1672

Sixteen-year-old Elizabeth Knapp, servant of Samuel Willard of Groton, Massachusetts, becomes "afflicted" and suffers until 1674 when she recovers, marries, and lives an ordinary, uneventful life. "Salem Farms" becomes the separate parish of Salem Village. James Bayley becomes the first preacher in Salem Village.

1680

George Burroughs succeeds Bayley as preacher in Salem Village.

1684

Deodat Lawson succeeds Burroughs as preacher in Salem Village.

1684–1686

King Charles II of England revokes the Massachusetts charter. King James II appoints Joseph Dudley president of New England. Sir Edmond Andros succeeds Dudley as president in 1686.

1688

The four children of John Goodwin (ages 13, 11, 7, 5) become "afflicted" in Boston. Mary Glover, mother of the Goodwin's laundress, is accused, confesses, and is executed for witchcraft.

1688–1691

Simon Bradstreet presides over the Massachusetts colony while negotiations for the new charter proceed.

1689

Samuel Parris succeeds Lawson as preacher of Salem Village church.

1691

Opponents of Reverend Parris assume control of the Salem Village council.

Late January/Early February 1692

Several young Salem Village girls begin exhibiting alarming symptoms.

February 19, 1692

The "afflicted" girls are diagnosed, reportedly by Dr. William Griggs, as suffering "under the Evil Hand."

February 25, 1692

Mary Sibley, aunt of Mary Walcott, engages the help of Reverend Parris's servants, Tituba and John Indian, to try counter-magic. They create a witch-cake which enrages Reverend Parris. Soon after, Elizabeth Parris, Abigail Williams, Elizabeth Hubbard, and Ann Putnam name their afflicters: Sarah Good, Sarah Osborne, and Tituba.

February 29–June 1, 1692

Arrests and Initial Hearings are presided over by Judges William Hathorne and Jonathan Corwin. Ultimately over 160 people are arrested. The spring arrests begin with Sarah Good and her infant, Sarah Osborne, and Tituba on February 29. March and April arrests include Martha and Giles Corey, Rebecca Nurse and her sisters, Sarah Cloyce and Mary Easty, and Elizabeth and John Proctor.

May 16, 1692

Sir William Phips is sworn in as Royal Governor of Massachusetts.

May 27, 1692
Governor Phips establishes the Court of Oyer and Terminer to handle the witchcraft cases. William Stoughton, Bartholomew Gedney, John Richards, Nathaniel Saltonstall, Wait Winthrop, Samuel Sewall, and Peter Sergeant are appointed to the court.

June 2–September 22, 1692
The Court of Oyer and Terminer holds trials; arrests continue; executions take place.

June 2, 1692
The Court of Oyer and Terminer convenes for the first time. One woman, Bridget Bishop, is convicted.

June 15, 1692
Nathaniel Saltonstall resigns from the Court of Oyer and Terminer. Jonathan Corwin takes his place on the bench.

June 30, 1692
The Court of Oyer and Terminer convenes for a second time. Five more women are convicted.

Early July 1692
Nathaniel Cary smuggles his wife Elizabeth Cary out of prison; Edward and Sarah Bishop flee; Philip and Mary English escape; John Alden disappears.

August 5, 1692
The Court of Oyer and Terminer convenes for a third time. Four men and two women are convicted.

September 9, 1692
The Court of Oyer and Terminer convenes for a fourth time. Six women are convicted.

September 17, 1692
The Court of Oyer and Terminer convenes for a fifth time. Seven women and two men are convicted.

September 19, 1692
Giles Corey is pressed to death.

October 1692
Many public petitions are sent to the court and there is open criticism of its procedures. "The Letter of Thomas Brattle," dated October 8, is circulated at this time.

October 29, 1692
The Court of Oyer and Terminer is dismissed by Governor Phips.

November 1692
Governor Phips releases many mothers and children from the jails.

December 16, 1692
The Superior Court of Judicature is formed. William Stoughton, Samuel Sewall, John Richards, Wait Winthrop, and Thomas Danforth are appointed to serve.

January–May 1693
The Superior Court of Judicature hears fifty-two cases; forty-nine defendants are acquitted or pardoned; three confess and are convicted. Governor Phips reprieves these three and issues a general pardon of others still in jail.

October 1693
Reverend Cotton Mather reassesses the trials in "The Wonders of the Invisible World."

November 26, 1694
Reverend Parris confesses to errors in conducting the witchcraft crisis; the anti-Parris contingent in Salem Village continues to withhold his salary.

January 14, 1695
Judge Samuel Sewall and twelve jurors publicly repent the actions of the Court of Oyer and Terminer which they had served.

July 1697
A panel of arbiters requires Salem Village to pay Reverend Parris 79 pounds, 9 shillings, and 6 pence. Parris and his daughter Elizabeth (Betty) leave for Stowe, Massachusetts.

1698
Reverend Joseph Green, who succeeded Parris as pastor of Salem Village Church, achieves a reconciliation of the Nurse and Putnam families.

1700
Robert Calef publishes an account of the Salem Witch Crisis, "More Wonders of the Invisible World," which includes an attack on both Increase Mather and Cotton Mather.

1702

Reverend John Hale publishes his account of the crisis, written in 1697, "A Modest Inquiry into the Nature of Witchcraft."

1706

Ann Putnam, now twenty-seven, confesses to delusion by the Devil.

1710

Nearly 600 pounds is distributed to families who claimed their property was unlawfully seized in 1692.

August 28, 1957

The Legislature of Massachusetts passes a bill clearing the names of all of the 1692 victims.

1991

A monument to the victims of the Salem Witch Trials is unveiled in Salem.

1992

The Salem monument is dedicated.

For Further Research

Salem Witchcraft Documents

Paul Boyer and Stephen Nissenbaum, eds., *Salem-Village Witchcraft: A Documentary Record of Local Conflict in Colonial New England*. Belmont, CA: Wadsworth Publishing Company, 1972.

——, *The Salem Witchcraft Papers: Verbatim Transcripts of the Legal Documents of the Salem Witchcraft Outbreak of 1692* in three volumes. New York: Da Capo Press, 1977.

George Lincoln Burr, ed., *Narratives of the Witchcraft Cases, 1648–1706* (1914). New York: Barnes & Noble, Inc., 1975 reprint. This volume includes "Remarkable Providences" by Increase Mather (1684); "Memorable Providences Relating to Witchcraft and Possession" by Cotton Mather (1689); "A Brief and True Narrative of Witchcraft at Salem Village" by Deodat Lawson (1692); "Letter of Thomas Brattle" (1692); Selections from "The Wonders of the Invisible World" by Cotton Mather (1693); Selections from "More Wonders of the Invisible World" by Robert Calef (1700); and "A Modest Inquiry into the Nature of Witchcraft" by John Hale (1702), among others.

About the Salem Witch Trials

Paul Boyer and Stephen Nissenbaum, *Salem Possessed: The Social Origins of Witchcraft*. Cambridge, MA: Harvard University Press, 1974.

Elaine G. Breslaw, *Tituba, Reluctant Witch of Salem: Devilish Indians and Puritan Fantasies*. New York and London: New York University Press, 1996.

David C. Brown, "The Case of Giles Cory," *Essex Institute Historical Collections*, vol. 12, no. 4, October 1985.

Linnda R. Caporael, "Ergotism: The Satan Loosed in Salem?" *Science*, vol. 192, April 2, 1976.

John Demos, *Entertaining Satan: Witchcraft and the Culture of Early New England*. New York: Oxford University Press, 1982.

Kai R. Erikson, *Wayward Puritans: A Study in the Sociology of Deviance*. New York: John Wiley and Sons, 1966.

Richard Godbeer, *The Devil's Dominion: Magic and Religion in Early New England*. Cambridge, England: Cambridge University Press, 1992.

Larry Gragg, *A Quest for Security: The Life of Samuel Parris 1653–1720*. Westport, CT: Greenwood Press, 1990.

———, *The Salem Witch Crisis*. Westport, CT: Greenwood Press, 1992.

Chadwick Hansen, *Witchcraft at Salem*. New York: George Braziller, Inc., 1969. Reprinted 1980.

David Harley, "Explaining Salem: Calvinist Psychology and the Diagnosis of Possession," *The American Historical Review*, vol. 101, no. 2, April 1996.

Nathaniel Hawthorne, *The House of the Seven Gables* (1851). New York: Penguin Books, 1981. Reprinted 1986.

Frances Hill, *A Delusion of Satan: The Full Story of the Salem Witch Trials*. New York: Doubleday, 1995.

Peter Charles Hoffer, *The Devil's Disciples: Makers of the Salem Witchcraft Trials*. Baltimore, MD: The Johns Hopkins University Press, 1996.

Carol F. Karlsen, *The Devil in the Shape of a Woman: Witchcraft in Colonial New England*. New York and London: W.W. Norton & Company, 1987.

George Lyman Kittredge, *Witchcraft in Old and New England*. Cambridge, MA: Harvard University Press, 1929.

Joseph Klaits, *Servants of Satan: The Age of the Witch Hunts*. Bloomington: Indiana University Press, 1985.

Bryan F. LeBeau, *The Story of the Salem Witch Trials*. Upper Saddle River, NJ: Prentice-Hall, Inc., 1998.

Brian P. Levack, *The Witch-Hunt in Early Modern Europe*. London: Longman Group UK Limited, 1987.

Alan Macfarlane, *Witchcraft in Tudor and Stuart England*. New York: Harper and Row, 1970.

Marc Mappen, ed., *Witches and Historians: Interpretations of Salem*. Malabar, FL: Krieger Publishing Company, 1980.

Arthur Miller, *The Crucible, a play in four acts* (1953). New York: Bantam, 1980.

Enders A. Robinson, *The Devil Discovered: Salem Witchcraft 1692*. New York: Hippocrene Books, 1991.

Bernard Rosenthal, *Salem Story: Reading the Witch Trials of 1692*. Cambridge, England: Cambridge University Press, 1993.

Samuel Sewall, *The Diary of Samuel Sewall*. Ed. M. Halsey Thomas. New York: Farrar, Straus & Giroux, Inc., 1973.

Nicholas P. Spanos and Jack Gottlieb, "Ergotism and the Salem Village Witch Trials," *Science*, vol. 194, December 24, 1976.

Marion L. Starkey, *The Devil in Massachusetts*. New York: Alfred A. Knopf, 1949.

Charles W. Upham, *Salem Witchcraft*. Boston: Wiggin and Lunt, 1867.

Richard Weisman, *Witchcraft, Magic, and Religion in 17th-Century Massachusetts*. Amherst: The University of Massachusetts Press, 1984.

John Winthrop, *The Journal of John Winthrop*. Eds. Richard S. Dunn, James Savage, and Laetitia Yeandle. Cambridge, MA: Belknap Press, 1996.

———, "A Model of Christian Charity," in *The Norton Anthology of American Literature*, shorter third edition. Nina Baym, general editor. New York: W.W. Norton & Company, 1999.

Videos

In Search of History: Salem Witch Trials. Executive Producers Robb Weller and Gary H. Grossman. A&E Television Networks, 1998. Distributed by New Video Group.

Secrets of the Dead: The Witches' Curse. Dir. Mark Lewis. Educational Broadcasting Corporation, 2001. Distributed by PBS Home Video.

Index